# Heroes

GREAT MEN
THROUGH THE AGES

# Heroes

### GREAT MEN THROUGH THE AGES

Written and Illustrated by

## Rebecca Hazell

ABBEVILLE PRESS PUBLISHERS

New York London Paris

# Contents

*For Chogyam Trungpa Mukpo, friend, teacher, and hero,*
*who taught me what heroism is.*

# Acknowledgments

Thank you to my husband, Mark, and children, Elisabeth and Stephan, for all their support and patience. Again, thanks to the many friends who contributed books and ideas to this project. A special thanks goes to the librarians of Halifax, in particular those of Captain William Spry Library, who went out of their way to be helpful. Last but not least, thanks go to my editors, Tessa Strickland and Meredith Wolf, to my mother, Doris Knotts, and to Kate Parker, my tireless and thorough copy editor.

First published in the United States of America in 1997 by Abbeville Publishing Group, 488 Madison Avenue, New York, N.Y. 10022. First published in Great Britain in 1996 by Barefoot Books Ltd., P.O. Box 95, Kingswood, Bristol BS15 5BH. Text and illustrations copyright © 1996 by Rebecca Hazell.

First edition
2 4 6 8 10 9 7 5 3 1

*For the American edition:*
Editor: Meredith Wolf
Jacket design: Celia Fuller
Production manager: Lou Bilka

*Library of Congress Cataloging-in-Publication Data*
Hazell, Rebecca.
    Heroes : great men through the ages / written and illustrated by Rebecca Hazell.
      p. cm.
    Includes bibliographical references.
    Summary: Profiles admirable men from around the world and throughout history, including Socrates, Prince Taishi Shōtoku, Leonardo da Vinci, William Shakespeare, Jorge Luis Borges, and Martin Luther King.
    ISBN 0-7892-0289-1
    1. Heroes—Biography—Juvenile literature. 2. Men Biography—Juvenile literature.
    [1. Heroes.] I. Title.
CT107.H39 1997
920.71—dc20                              96—36467

*(BAL 4146) Proportions of the human figure, c. 1492 (Vitruvian Man) by Leonardo da Vinci (1452–1519) (p. 28) reproduced courtesy of Galleria dell'Accademia, Venice/Bridgeman Art Library, London.*

# Introduction

Do you ever wish you could visit faraway places or travel back in time? In fact you can do these things every time you open a history book. History is made up of stories of people like you and me, leading their lives and having adventures at any time in the past.

Many history books only tell about governments, wars, and dates. These facts are important, but if you are like me, you want to imagine what it felt like to live in a world quite different from our own. This is what I tried to do when I wrote this book, which is about several historical people who were all heroes in their own way. You might think of heroes as brave leaders, fearless warriors, daring rescuers, or even sports champions. But my idea of a hero is not limited to these kinds of people. I think a hero is anyone who is brave, kind, or wise—not just once but for an entire lifetime.

In this book you will find many kinds of heroes, from all around the world and from different periods of history. Some were great warriors or rulers, and others were artists, scientists, authors, or philosophers. All of them did things that affect our world today. Although these men made mistakes like anyone else, and although some of them had talents that were not properly recognized in their own day, each used his talents fully, with courage and conviction to the benefit of others.

There are many more heroic people than could fit into these pages. There are heroes— and heroines—living around us all over the world, but there just isn't room for everyone in a single book. Who else might you include?

The story of each hero is illustrated with his portrait, other scenes from his lifetime, and a map of the area in which he lived. I have tried to draw each man just as someone living in his own time might have done. I hope that the stories and illustrations in this book will make you think of heroes of your own and will inspire you to use your own special talents to be heroic in your own way.

Rebecca Hazell

# Socrates

*Greece, circa 470–399 B.C.*

About 2,400 years ago, in the Greek city-state of Athens, a stonemason named Socrates began a quest for the truth. When he was a young man, while bravely serving in his city's army, a fellow soldier found Socrates standing immobile next to his tent. For many hours nothing could be done to break his strange concentration.

Socrates never told anyone what had happened to him that day, but when his army duties were over, he began to question why the world exists. Eventually he stopped working and began studying to find an answer to his question. He looked to science for an answer but had no success. He wanted to know more than *how* things work—he wanted to know *why;* he sought to learn the purpose of life. Since everyone gave a different answer to his question, Socrates decided to find his own answer.

Socrates began by asking himself what people are like and what they desire. He saw that everyone wanted happiness. He also saw that people often believed, mistakenly, that pleasure, power, or success would make them happy, even though many who already had these things were still unhappy. He concluded that these things were false sources of happiness, and that until people found what was true and good, they could not be happy. This meant they had to search within themselves to separate the false from the true. To Socrates the purpose of life and the path to happiness were to live the truth.

As he grew older, Socrates spent his days holding conversations at the agora, or marketplace, where ideas and goods were exchanged. Through his talks with young men, politicians, and other philosophers, Socrates became known as the wisest man of his day. Yet he asserted that he knew only that he did not know, while others pretended to possess wisdom they did not really have.

Socrates's motto was, "The unexamined life is not worth living." He took nothing on faith, but rather, inquired into each person's beliefs. Through logic and with humor, he helped them see what they did not know so that they could recognize truth for themselves. He questioned anyone and everyone in this way. Unfortunately, some people did not want their opinions questioned, and Socrates made many enemies.

Athens had been a great power in Greece when Socrates was young, but by the time he was an old man, war, plague, and political unrest troubled the city. Angry politicians, unhappy with his ceaseless questions, arrested him, charging him with demoralizing young

ΣΟΚΡΑΤΗΣ

9

people and slandering the gods. They thought he would escape to another city, be discredited, and stop bothering them. Socrates knew that once he had been arrested, he would be tried and convicted by a frightened mob. Yet he also knew that if he ran away, he would betray both his beloved Athens and his own teachings about living the truth. So, instead of fleeing, he chose to stay and face his certain penalty, death.

The way in which Socrates accepted his death immortalized him. Two of his students, Plato and Xenophon, wrote famous descriptions of his life, his teaching methods, and his courageous end. Socrates is remembered for humor and integrity, and his pursuit of truth became the foundation for Western philosophy.

## ATHENS'S BRIEF GLORY

Ancient Greece was a series of smaller city-states rather than one united country. These city-states shared the same language and worshiped the same gods, but each had a different form of government. Citizens of each city-state were deeply loyal to their own community and suspicious of others.

Around 505 B.C., Athens developed a form of government known as direct democracy. Rather than electing representatives, each citizen (a status denied to women, slaves, and foreigners) could vote directly on what Athens should do. For a while, this kind of government worked well, but in time Athenian democracy ran into some big problems.

Difficulties arose after the great Persian empire invaded Greece around

*All Greeks idealized the heroic warrior; Socrates became the ideal of the heroic philosopher.*

490 B.C. The Greek city-states always had a hard time getting along with each other and were able to form an alliance only when threatened. Together they fought bravely against the Persian invaders, but after Athens led them to victory in 449 B.C., the other city-states resented Athens's leadership. They had good reason, for Athens soon slipped into imperialism. Originally all of the city-states had contributed money to a treasury for their common defense. But after the Persian defeat, the leaders of Athens seized this money (called tributes), saying that they were again in danger of invasion and demanded even more.

While Athens prospered, its citizens were happy. They reelected the same leader, Pericles, again and again. Pericles had a great vision for his city. He wanted it to lead Greece in peace as well as war and to be a center for culture and art. After the Persian wars, he set its craftsmen and artists to work creating great public monuments and temples. The grandest and most beautiful was the Parthenon, dedicated to Athens's patron goddess, Athena. Socrates (a stone-mason by training) probably helped build it. At the same time drama, poetry, philosophy, and science flourished. Athens did become the center of Greek culture, but it was at the expense of its neighbors, whose tributes paid for its rise.

*The Parthenon—standing atop the massive hill known as the Acropolis—contained a gigantic statue of Athena, goddess of wisdom.*

This Athenian "golden age" could not last. Led by Athens's old rival, Sparta, the other city-states took their revenge. Athens's power slowly crumbled as it had to face repeated invasions, sieges, plagues, and famines. Its democracy crumbled too. No one could agree on how to defend the city. The people were easily swayed by any convincing speaker. Fear, not good sense, lay behind their votes and twice, small groups of powerful men used their private armies to take over the government and terrorize their own people. By the time democracy was restored, Athens had changed. Its citizens craved security, not freedom of thought, and the search for truth, like that of Socrates, was no longer valued.

The elderly Socrates became a victim of this new mentality, and his style of questioning was criticized. Socrates understood the fear people felt. He knew it made them weak. At his trial, he refused to rely on grandiose speeches or to beg for pity in order to sway their emotions. Instead he told them that he had been Athens's gadfly of truth, whose questioning had roused its citizens out of their stupidity and greed. Expecting to be voted guilty by all, he was able to sway some jurors and was condemned by only a narrow majority.

## COURAGE TO THE END

It was an Athenian tradition to ask a condemned man what his punishment should be. At the end of Socrates's trial, he answered that instead of being punished, he should be given free dinners for the rest of his life! His lack of seriousness angered the citizens, and they voted to give him the death sentence. There was no appeal.

While he awaited his execution, Socrates was urged by his friends to escape. They offered to bribe his jailer, but he refused to leave. First, he knew that he would be discredited if he fled. He also believed in obeying the laws of the land, even when they were unjust. He was certain that his death would be a greater gift to his community than his living, for by dying he would preserve his integrity and possibly serve as an example to others.

As Socrates waited in jail, his friends continued to visit him to discuss philosophy. When the day came for him to die, his jailers gave him a poisoned drink made from hemlock root. He drank it without hesitating. Surrounded by weeping friends, Socrates talked calmly as the poison took effect. He found himself comforting them until he died.

One of his students, Plato, described not only Socrates's passing but also his life in a series of question-and-answer dialogues. Plato later became as famous as his teacher. No one is quite sure whether Plato's biography tells us more about Socrates's philosophy or about his own, but what Plato does make clear is how wise, courageous, humorous, and beloved his teacher had been. Socrates remained loyal to his community to the end. Perhaps he foresaw that it would someday extend beyond Athens to include all seekers of wisdom.

# GREECE IN THE 6TH–4TH CENTURIES B.C.

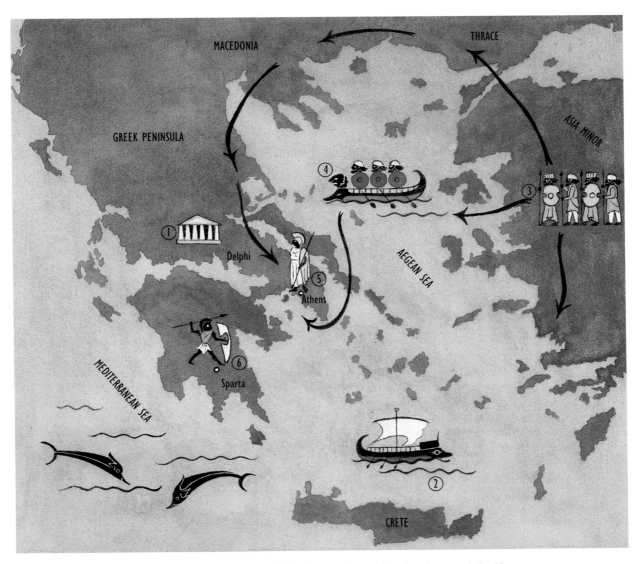

1. In ancient Greece, one of the major religious shrines was at Delphi, where a priestess delivered oracles—prophetic visions.

2. The ancient Greeks populated many islands in the Aegean and Mediterranean seas, had colonies in Italy and Asia Minor, and traded with other countries along the coast of the Mediterranean.

3. In the late sixth century B.C., the mighty Persian empire conquered the Greek cities in Asia Minor, followed by Thrace, Macedonia, and finally mainland Greece itself.

4. Persia twice tried to conquer Greece, but its little city-states combined forces to defeat the huge Persian navy.

5. Although the Persians burned Athens, the city not only escaped complete destruction but, after extensive rebuilding, emerged more beautiful than ever.

6. Sparta led the other city-states in defeating Athens, thus bringing to an end a golden age for the arts in ancient Greece.

# Prince Taishi Shōtoku

*Japan, A.D. 574–622*

Thirteen hundred years ago, Japan was a rustic island empire on the eastern edge of Asia. Its rulers claimed to be descended from the sun goddess, Amaterasu. Although these leaders were worshiped almost as gods by the masses, they were often powerless against ambitious wealthy nobles. Because there was no clear way to choose a new ruler when an emperor or empress died, civil war often broke out between rival clans, causing suffering for the whole nation. In 593 these clans were able to agree upon a new empress, a member of the most powerful clan. However, she was a mere figurehead, since the real power was held by her nephew, Prince Taishi Shōtoku, who was married to a woman from another influential clan.

When Prince Shōtoku became regent of Japan, he was only nineteen years old. Unlike many rulers, this remarkable young man was not interested in power for its own sake; he wanted to help his country. To do this he had to keep the rival clans at peace with each other while promoting Japan's prosperity.

Prince Shōtoku knew that Japan's political institutions were not very sophisticated, so as the Japanese had done in the past, he looked far over the sea to China for inspiration. First he reformed and centralized his government based on the teachings of the Chinese sage Confucius. Confucius taught that everyone must be responsible for one another's welfare. He said that governments should be run by able people regardless of their background, and not only people who had inherited power, as had been the case in Japan. Inspired by these ideals, Prince Shōtoku persuaded the ambitious nobles to give up some of their powers to capable commoners, a policy that improved the efficiency and quality of Japanese government. The prince also introduced the Chinese calendar and writing system to Japan.

Then the prince sent out messengers across five hundred miles of stormy seas to study Chinese culture. They brought back many artists, craftsmen, and scholars. From them Japanese artists and craftsmen learned new skills that they adapted to form a brilliant new culture. Prince Shōtoku did still more for his people. He built highways and irrigation systems. He started social programs. He erected temples and established a new court near the city of Nara. (These buildings are among the oldest surviving wooden structures on earth.) The prince also wrote a history of Japan, which sadly no longer survives.

Prince Shōtoku also helped spread a new religion, Buddhism. Until this time, the Japanese religion, called Shinto, was based on rituals that showed love and respect for nature. Buddhism taught people a way of life based on caring for each other as well. Buddhism did not replace Shinto—the Japanese practiced both religions, as they still do today—but it did deeply affect the way people lived. Buddhist values of compassion helped reduce the amount of violence in Japanese society.

Sometimes people do not like change, but the Japanese welcomed Prince Shōtoku's improvements. During his reign, Japan became more peaceful and prosperous. Its contact with the Chinese enriched and stimulated its culture. The changes Prince Shōtoku brought to Japan continue to affect its history and even now, the Japanese honor him as a great Buddhist saint.

*Japan evolved its own traditions, such as* kyudo, *a form of archery based upon meditation.*

## A NEW CULTURE

Although Japan borrowed many ideas from China, its people soon adapted them to their own ways. During Prince Shōtoku's reign, new forms of architecture, music, sculpture, painting, textile design, and dance developed. Some still flourish in their ancient form, such as gagaku, a type of Japanese dance.

The Japanese also created their own unique art forms, expressed in mediums such as wood-block prints, paper, and fabrics, that are now world famous, like origami, the Japanese art of paper folding. Japanese Buddhists developed other art forms like the tea ceremony, flower arranging, and archery as well. Each combines a simple activity with strict discipline to create an atmosphere of simplicity and calm.

Eventually, the Japanese integrated Chinese writing symbols (kanji) with their own traditional script (hiragana). They loved calligraphy (decorative handwriting) and wrote masterful poetry and novels. One type of poetry, the haiku, has only seventeen syllables, yet can make its readers see, hear, and feel as the poet does and has inspired poets around the world.

Many of the arts that flowered during the reign of Prince Shōtoku are still practiced in Japan today. The present imperial family is descended from the prince and the other early "divine" rulers, making it the longest unbroken line of rulers in the world.

## PRINCE AND SAINT

We know little about what Prince Shōtoku was like as a person. He became regent because both he and his wife were related to the most important rival clans. But he was also probably chosen because people admired him. His actions tell us that he was courageous, kind, and diplomatic. He cared for everyone in his country and gave them a vision to follow.

*Prince Shōtoku brought peace and prosperity to all levels of Japanese society by borrowing ideas from Chinese culture.*

When Prince Shōtoku sent his messengers to China, students, artisans, merchants, and scholars went too. In those days a voyage of five hundred miles was as dangerous as a trip to the moon would be today. Finding the route must have been difficult, because the pilots had no compasses to guide them. If they came too close to land on the way, pirates lay in wait for them. On the open sea where even pirates feared to roam, they had to brave terrible storms in which many ships were lost. Yet the travelers must have felt that they were sharing not only an adventure but a mission to create a better Japan. It was the prince who gave them that sense of mission.

Through his reforms and his encouragement, Prince Shōtoku changed the way the Japanese people thought as well as the way they lived. During his lifetime he persuaded the wealthy, ambitious nobles to stop fighting one another while he set about improving the lives of ordinary people. And when he adopted Buddhism, he taught the Japanese a way to care for each other as well as for their beautiful world. They all seem to have loved him.

After Prince Shōtoku's death in 622, the great clans again fought for power. The prince's own sons were murdered in the conflict. But his reforms survived the strife. Within a few years, new leaders, also related to him, made sure that they took hold. The prince himself was immortalized as the father of Japanese culture. Some people change the world through force and fear, but not Prince Shōtoku. The Japanese people called him a saint because of both the good things he did for Japan and because he had a great heart.

# JAPAN AND CHINA AROUND THE 4TH–7TH CENTURIES A.D.

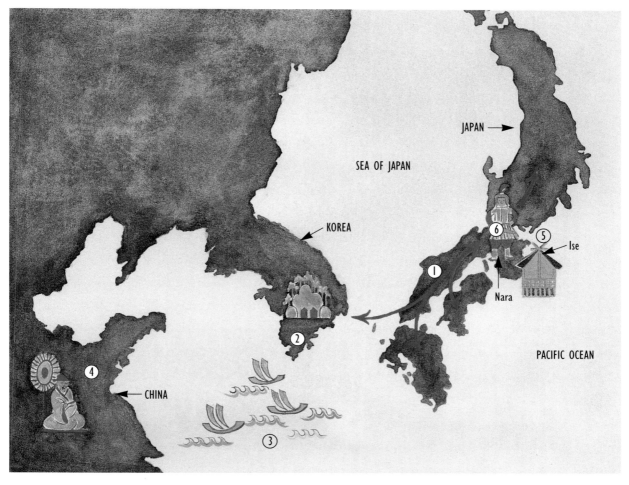

1. Waves of settlers, many coming through Korea, had spread into Japan for centuries before Prince Shōtoku came to power.

2. After the early clans had colonized Japan, they spread back to the Asian mainland, conquering part of southern Korea.

3. Prince Shōtoku's fleet of ships avoided Korea, where it no longer had a foothold, and made the longer and more dangerous journey to China.

4. China's emperor thought it only natural that Japan would want to copy his country, but the Japanese adapted Chinese ideas to their own use.

5. The early Japanese rulers claimed descent from the sun goddess, Amaterasu. Her main shrine, still the most important in Japan, is at Ise.

6. Prince Shōtoku established his court near Nara, in central Japan.

# Mansa Kankan Musa

*West Africa, ?–1342 or 1347*

In 1324, a great Muslim emperor arrived in Egypt from Mali in West Africa. Mansa Musa, or "Emperor Moses," was on a pilgrimage to the holy city of Mecca in Arabia. His journey took about a year, since his empire was thousands of miles away. About eighty thousand people came with him, including slaves, servants, warriors, and wives. They rode camels or horses, or they walked in ranks carrying solid gold batons.

Mansa Musa also brought with him some 150 tons of gold as spending money. He visited Cairo, where he spent and gave away so much gold that its value remained lowered for years. He was so devout that he preferred visiting mosques to paying his respects to the sultan of Egypt and had to be persuaded to call on the sultan before he gave offense. Everywhere they went, he and his retinue impressed people with their good manners and generosity.

Through trade, Mansa Musa's gold and his name made their way to Europe. Africa was then a mystery to Europeans. They thought it was full of terrifying monsters. The vast Sahara Desert and the unfriendly Islamic countries of North Africa kept them out, but it was Mansa Musa who changed their picture of Africa. For centuries after his rule, merchants and adventurers tried to find a direct route to the source of his marvelous wealth.

Mansa Musa became legendary in West Africa for his wisdom as well as his wealth. He ruled the second-largest empire in the world, stretching from the Atlantic Ocean in the west to grasslands in the east, and from the Sahara Desert in the north to jungles in the south. (Only the Mongol empire of Asia was larger.) He held absolute power over many tribes with differing languages, customs, and religions.

Mansa Musa made cities like Timbuktu into famous trading centers. Their merchants took gold, ivory, copper, salt, and cola nuts away in long caravans. They crossed the Sahara Desert and returned months later with fabrics, horses, swords, knives, books, and precious writing paper. Within Mali, craftsmen, weavers, tailors, and metalsmiths in the cities traded with artisans, farmers, and fishermen from the countryside. Everyone prospered.

As emperor, Mansa Musa could have fulfilled his every desire. Instead, he chose to use his resources for the benefit of his people. He made sure all his subjects were safe and well governed. He encouraged them to be creative and to respect one another.

With so much power, Mansa Musa could have been greedy or cruel, like so many other rulers have been. But this great king wanted the best for his subjects. Instead of provoking

fear, he inspired love and respect. Long after his death, he was remembered as a leader who put his people first.

## FABULOUS KINGDOMS

African gold stirred the curiosity and greed of European adventurers. Looking for its famous wealth, they explored Africa's coastline but found few paths into its heartland. Later, Europeans and North and South Americans created wealth for themselves by selling African slaves in Europe and then in the Americas. They learned little about Africa itself, treated their captives worse than they did animals, and created a picture in their minds of an inferior black race with no history and no culture.

Nothing could have been less true. Africa had its own history, as rich and full as any on earth. Mansa Musa's fabulous empire was part of that history. It was the second of three great empires—Ghana, Mali, and Songhai—that arose in western Africa, south of

*The great cities of the Mali empire have faded away, although Timbuktu is still characterized by the type of architecture introduced by Mansa Musa's architects.*

the Sahara Desert. Mali was founded in the thirteenth century by the great "Hungering Lion," Sundiata, after he had defeated the oppressive ruler of the last remnant of the Ghana empire. Sundiata became one of West Africa's greatest heroes because he brought not only victory but well-being to his subjects.

Mansa Musa was Sundiata's descendant. The Mali empire was in trouble by the time that Mansa Musa came to power. Some of the emperors after Sundiata had been weak and greedy, and one had even been viciously insane. Mansa Musa took charge of his people. To gain control over most of West Africa, he used diplomacy where he could and war where he needed it. He established a government that did not get bogged down in the tribal conflicts that could tear an empire apart. His officials were honest. He made sure that people could travel safely anywhere in Mali and be met with hospitality.

*Almost nothing of Mansa Musa's empire has survived. A few statues, including this figure, have been found in the remains of the city of Djenné.*

When Mansa Musa returned from Mecca, he brought back advisers, scholars, and even a famous architect who created a new kind of architecture for the emperor's building projects. He constructed mosques and public buildings in his cities, and he founded a university in Timbuktu. As learning spread throughout the empire, Mali became famous throughout the Muslim world as an important center of education and wisdom. In contrast, contemporary Europeans were facing the twin disasters of plague and war.

*Mansa Musa might have witnessed traditional tribal dances during which headdresses such as this were worn.*

## THE SACRED EMPEROR

We are still learning about life in the empire of Mansa Musa, but there is no doubt that he was the center of its existence. He was evidently not only a competent ruler and general but also a joyous and generous person. When his armies conquered new lands, he did not depose the former kings. Instead, he allowed them to stay in power under him. To make sure they remained loyal and just, however, he took their sons home as hostages. Then he raised them as his own and even made some of them generals. He aimed to bring out the best in those around him.

Mansa Musa's main concern was that all his subjects be treated fairly. He was both the lawmaker and the supreme court of his society, and anyone had the right to appeal to him for justice. At the same time, he was not someone to be approached casually. The emperor was sacred to his people. As the highest-ranking man in the land, he was surrounded by splendor. Royal musicians announced his entry. The best horses and warriors were on hand to await his commands. When he held court, he sat under a huge silk umbrella, carried by one of his Turkish slaves, and wore voluminous silk trousers. On either side of him stood two huge elephant tusks. His solid gold bow, arrows, sword, and spear rested nearby. Next to him was the royal executioner, ready to mete out justice on the spot.

When his subjects approached him, they knelt and sprinkled dust on their heads as a mark of respect. Then they could speak their business. Mansa Musa rarely addressed his subjects directly. His orders always went through his spokesman. In fact, he was so sacred that no one was even allowed to see him eat. His senior wife brought him food and left. Only then would this mighty emperor, seated on elegant cushions and carpets and surrounded by silk hangings, begin his meal, all alone.

# MANSA MUSA'S AFRICA

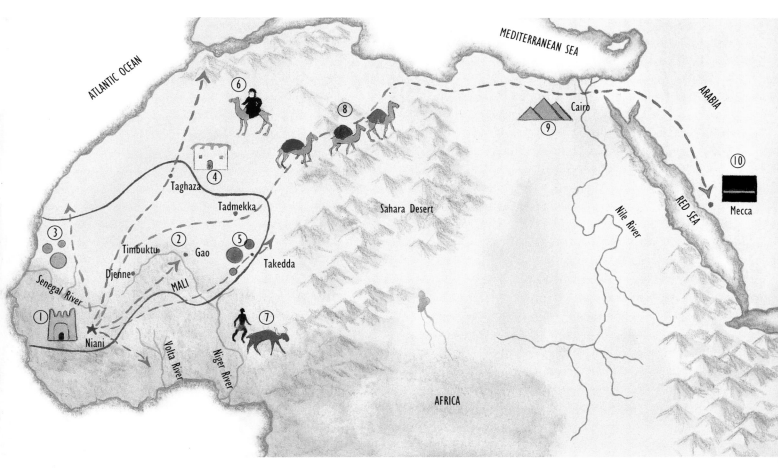

- - -    SOME OF THE MANY TRADE ROUTES USED BY THE MERCHANTS OF MALI
- - -    ROUTE OF MANSA MUSA'S PILGRIMAGE TO MECCA

1. Mansa Musa's capital was at Niani. Little remains of it now.
2. Major trading cities like Djenné, Timbuktu, Gao, and Tadmekka linked Mali with the rest of Africa.
3. Gold was mined in this area, but the location of the mines was always kept secret. Today most of the gold is gone, dispersed around the world.
4. Mali's wealth depended on salt as much as on gold. This was mined in the desert, in a city where even the houses were built of blocks of salt.
5. Another source of Mali's wealth was copper, mined at Takedda.
6. Members of the nomadic Tuareg tribe led most of the caravans across the Sahara Desert. They gave allegiance to the empire of Mali.
7. Other tribes within the empire herded cattle, farmed, or specialized in crafts such as weaving or pottery.
8. Mansa Musa's long pilgrimage to Mecca was difficult and dangerous, yet thousands of people joined him.
9. Once the center of a great Egyptian empire, Cairo was part of the Islamic world by the time of Mansa Musa. He would have passed the pyramids, already ancient in his day.
10. In Mecca, Mansa Musa would have visited the Kaaba, the holiest shrine in the Muslim world.

# Leonardo da Vinci

*Italy, 1452–1519*

Leonardo da Vinci may have been the greatest genius in history. An artist, scientist, engineer, architect, inventor, and musician, he came to symbolize his era—the Italian Renaissance. Although he was courted by royalty, few people then fully appreciated the true breadth of his genius because many of his ideas were centuries ahead of their time.

Leonardo was born in 1452 in Vinci, Italy. Early on, his family realized how bright, curious, and talented he was. Even as a child, he could already use both his left and right hands equally well. Leonardo's parents apprenticed him to Verrocchio, a leading artist in nearby Florence, to learn a trade. There Leonardo studied painting, sculpture, music, mathematics, and science and worked on projects including painting, sculpture, and architecture with other students. By the time Leonardo was an adult, he was already a famous artist and musician.

When Leonardo was still a young man, he moved to Milan, then one of the five great Italian city-states. His patron, or employer, was Ludovico Sforza—the city's ruler. Leonardo worked in Milan for many years not only as an artist and musician but also as an engineer, inventor, and producer of pageants and parades. His paintings revolutionized the art world; until then, most art had been used to illustrate religious themes. It was often stylized and lifeless, but by contrast Leonardo's paintings revealed a meaningful and realistic world. Artists from all over Europe came to Milan to study them.

Many people also regard Leonardo as the first modern scientist, because he observed the world in detail and sought explanations about why things happened; to him there was no separation between art and science. He filled many notebooks with his ideas, drawing and writing down his observations about nature. He studied plants, animals, anatomy, and the flight of birds; he observed the patterns of water and wind, light and shadow, and the movement of heavenly bodies. On paper he "invented" airplanes, armored tanks, paddleboats, and many other mechanical devices that did not become reality until modern times. To keep his notes private, he wrote backward. To read them, someone had to hold his notes in front of a mirror!

Despite his great creativity, Leonardo never completed some of his projects, and others began to fall apart soon after they were finished. His famous wall painting *The Last Supper* started to disintegrate almost at once because of the new paint formula he had tried. His curiosity often led him from one thing to another before he had completed the first. He always intended to come back and finish a project, but often another good idea would pop up

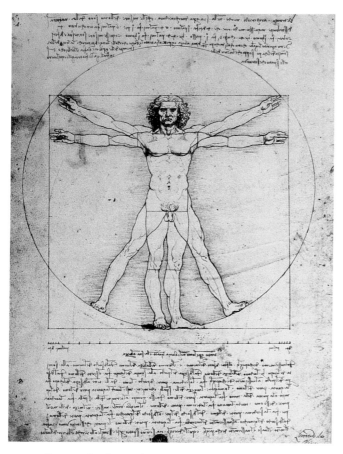

*Leonardo drew this famous diagram, which mathematically represents the proportions of the human body, for a friend's book.*

and he would begin work on that instead. And sometimes war interrupted his work.

In 1499, Milan was invaded by France. Leonardo left the city and spent several years working in one Italian city-state after another. In Mantua a noblewoman, Isabelle d'Este, asked him to paint her portrait. He never did, but her numerous letters to him tell us much about his life and work that we would not have known otherwise.

Leonardo discovered new things wherever he went, while all around him countries and cities were fighting and destroying each other. Once he was commissioned to inspect fortifications for one of Italy's most ruthless tyrants, Cesare Borgia. Borgia in fact was so bloodthirsty that Leonardo finally quit the job. Fortunately, Borgia ignored Leonardo's ideas for making better weapons, such as cannon that could fire exploding cannonballs.

Leonardo was never able to settle down and concentrate on any one project for very long, and the frequent wars in Italy made no sense to him. While he was often commissioned to design weapons and defense systems—work that he enjoyed because he never could resist a chance to explore some of his ideas—he found war itself "a bestial madness." He foresaw that the "arms race" of his own time would only cause increasing trouble for humankind. In one of his notebooks he wrote, "Ambitious people, never content with the world's gifts of life and beauty, ruin their own lives and can never benefit from the utility and beauty of the world."

Getting older and growing tired, Leonardo tried working for the pope in Rome, where all the best artists were flocking. However, there his younger rivals, like Sandro Botticelli, Domenico Ghirlandaio, Raphael, and Michelangelo, were being given work that would previously have been offered to him.

As an old man, Leonardo moved to France to work for King Francis I. He spent his last years there, working on his ideas and entertaining the king. His notes filled thousands of pages. He had hoped they would be published immediately after his death to benefit humanity. Instead, they were hidden in collections across Europe, where no one had access to them for three hundred years. By then, many of his observations had been made by others. Had they been available sooner, the entire history of Western science might have been quite different.

Many of Leonardo's paintings were also lost, although today we can see those that have survived in museums around the world and even on the internet, where we can visit the Leonardo da Vinci Virtual Museum. We can also see some of his ideas—from helicopters to diving suits—that have been brought to life.

## THE RENAISSANCE

Leonardo was born at an exciting time. All across Europe, people were dropping old ways of thinking and acting. For centuries the church had taught that life was full of nothing but sin, death, and judgment. But now people began to celebrate life and to value their human qualities. Ancient Greek science and philosophy, with their emphasis on rational thought, came to light. Through the study of mathematics, philosophy, geography, and astronomy, people began examining the world around them and what lay beyond it. The newly developed printed books spread ideas everywhere. Explorers seeking wealth crossed land and sea. With so many new discoveries, this period came to be called the Renaissance, or "rebirth."

However, these times were also difficult. In Europe, countries and cities were often at war. In Italy, city-states were often ruled by tyrannical and devious men. Republican Florence was lucky to have fairly decent

*Leonardo studied birds carefully, observing aspects of their flight that were not confirmed until the invention of the slow-motion camera.*

leaders, however. Proud of their city, artists like Leonardo helped make it beautiful. But Florence also had to play power politics with other city-states. In fact Leonardo's move to Milan was probably an attempt to improve relations between the two cities.

After leaving Milan, Leonardo received many commissions around Italy, ranging from painting portraits and battle scenes to designing cannons and drainage and canal systems. One commission was for the portrait now called the Mona Lisa, most likely the most famous painting in history. But Leonardo did not wait for a commission to explore new ideas. For instance, because he believed that plague struck when people lived too close together (and indeed crowded conditions did contribute to the spread of disease), he designed the first spacious "suburbs." He tried to persuade the sultan of Turkey to hire him to build the longest and highest bridge in the world. He applied mathematical principles to everything, from music and art to the flight of cannonballs. He drew beautiful and accurate maps. Wherever he went, Leonardo was welcomed as the ideal Renaissance man because he was good at so many different things.

## LONELY GENIUS

When Leonardo was young, he was strong, handsome, witty, and popular, and was known to be a practical joker. It would have been fun to take walks with him, as he was interested in everything he saw. He liked to explore the countryside, poking into caves or settling down on a hilltop to draw the rivers and valleys below.

Leonardo loved all animals but especially horses, and he drew beautiful sketches of them. One of his greatest disappointments was a failed project to cast in bronze a statue of a twenty-four-foot-high horse. He had made a spectacular full-size clay model for it, which was on public display. But the bronze he was to use was shipped away to make cannons for battle. During the war, soldiers used the model for target practice, destroying it.

As Leonardo grew older, he withdrew into himself. People admired him, but they did not understand him. While other Renaissance thinkers believed that the earth and everything on it were for everyone's use, Leonardo felt that people were just as much subject to nature's laws as were animals, plants, or the weather. Others considered the human being to be "the measure of all things"—more important than anything else—but he saw humans as just small players on the huge stage of existence.

Although Leonardo remained a generous teacher, inventor, and thinker until the end of his life, it seems that he grew increasingly lonely. Perhaps he felt disappointed in his fellow people, whose appetite for war never ended, whose imaginations could never match his own, and who could never seem to appreciate the wonderful world in quite the same way he did.

# LEONARDO'S ITALY

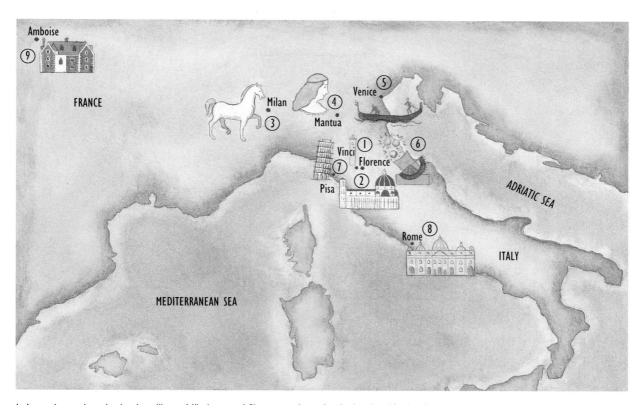

1. Leonardo was born in the tiny village of Vinci, west of Florence, and was baptized under this church tower.

2. Leonardo was apprenticed to the artist Verrocchio in Florence. He may have helped his teacher design a golden ball to be placed on top of the huge dome of the Cathedral of Santa Maria del Fiore.

3. In his early twenties, Leonardo moved to Milan. There he painted *The Last Supper* and began the great horse sculpture that was never cast in bronze.

4. After France invaded Milan, Leonardo briefly visited Mantua, where Isabelle d'Este demanded that he paint her portrait, a request that remained unfulfilled.

5. Leonardo visited Venice, where its leaders asked him for advice on how to defend their city.

6. One of the many patrons to court Leonardo in and around Florence was the warlike tyrant Cesare Borgia.

7. Leonardo was also asked to help Florence in its siege of Pisa, whose famous tower did not lean as much in those days as it does today.

8. Leonardo even tried working for the pope in Rome, but newer and younger artists were given the commissions instead.

9. Leonardo crossed the Alps to be the guest of the king of France at Amboise. Here Leonardo was respected and well cared for, and it was here that he eventually died.

# William Shakespeare

*England, 1564–1616*

About four hundred years ago, when William Shakespeare began writing and performing plays for his fellow Englishmen, he did not know that he would become the greatest English-language playwright in history. He just wanted to entertain people.

Shakespeare was born in Stratford-upon-Avon in 1564. William received a good basic education, but he also learned by observing the world around him. He had an eye for detail, an ear for the rhythms of speech, and a quick mind. As a newly married young man, he left his wife and children at home and set off for London to try his fortune in the theater.

Plays were increasingly popular in those days. Earlier religious plays had given way to performances full of action, violence, and romance. Actors and playwrights were in great demand. Shakespeare showed he could be both, becoming one of London's favorites.

When plague broke out in London in 1593, theaters had to shut down, and acting troupes fled to the countryside. There they toured about, spreading the popularity of Shakespeare's plays. During this time, Shakespeare began to write poetry, creating some of the most beautiful and mysterious poems in the English language. He cleverly dedicated some of them to a wealthy noble, who rewarded him generously. When the plague died down, Shakespeare used this money to buy a part ownership of The Globe, a theater near London. He now received income as an actor, as an author, and as a theater owner.

Shakespeare's actors called themselves the "Lord Chamberlain's Men," using the title of the powerful noble who had become their patron. His plays were even performed for Queen Elizabeth I. Shakespeare himself probably acted in some of them. After the queen's death, the new ruler, King James I, liked Shakespeare's plays and acting company so well that he became their patron, and the troupe then became known as the "King's Men."

Shakespeare eventually grew wealthy and retired, returning to his family in Stratford. He wrote a few more plays, but he enjoyed life in the country too much to return to London. He died surrounded by loving family and friends.

Tragically, Shakespeare's plays were nearly lost. He never published them during his lifetime for fear they would fall into a rival troupe's hands. Without the devotion of his friends, Shakespeare's work might have been forgotten. But they realized he had written timeless plays of true genius. After his death, two good friends from his acting company reconstructed his plays from memory, notes, and some inferior pirated versions used by rival companies.

They put them together in a collection and had them published. In the introduction to the volume, his famous friend and fellow playwright Ben Jonson wrote, "He was not for an age but for all time."

## "ALL THE WORLD'S A STAGE"

In Shakespeare's day, the public theaters looked somewhat like inn courtyards, which is where early plays had often been held. The plays could only be performed during daylight, when the weather was good. On performance days a trumpet blast and a flag fluttering over the theater attracted theatergoers.

The stage jutted out into the audience and was known as an "apron." It was sometimes covered with a sort of attic, so that actors could be let down by ropes if the script called for a god to descend from above. A trap door in the stage floor allowed actors to rise from underneath also. The attic was nicknamed "heaven" and the area beneath the stage was "hell." There were no realistic sets. One bush might represent a whole forest, or someone might carry a sign on stage describing where the scene was taking place.

*Did The Globe Theatre look like this?*

Wealthy spectators sat in tiers of booths all around the stage, while common folk stood on the ground under the open sky. Some audience members even paid extra to sit on the stage itself. People expected to be entertained, and they threw garbage at the performers if they were not!

*. . . or like this. The only two pictures of it disagree.*

All the actors were either men or young boys with high voices and without beards. Boys played the female roles because acting was considered to be too coarse of a profession for women. The actors wore rich costumes that once had belonged to the nobility. However, these costumes rarely matched the play's setting. Instead, for a play set in ancient Greece, one actor might wear a piece of armor that looked vaguely antique. The audience had to supply other details from their own imaginations.

Because the sets and costumes were not realistic, props and sound effects were very important. For instance, during fight scenes an actor carried a pig's bladder filled with blood under his clothes. When he was "stabbed," he would "bleed" realistically. The audience loved it! For the sound of thunder, someone rolled cannonballs around in "heaven." Cannon were fired during battle scenes too. Once in fact, the shot from the cannon set Shakespeare's theater on fire and burned it to the ground!

Shakespeare's plays were perfect for the audiences and theaters of his time. Knowing that plays were equally popular with the wealthy and the ordinary people, he learned how to appeal to them all. With unrealistic costumes and sets, and no breaks for scene changes, the action and dialogue had to stir people's imaginations. Shakespeare's plays were filled with rich images from nature and daily life that allowed people to understand the action more clearly.

*Shakespeare's acting troupe often performed in the homes of nobles as well as in theaters.*

During Shakespeare's lifetime, England was enjoying the Elizabethan Renaissance, named after Queen Elizabeth I. She herself was especially fond of plays. Shakespeare happily included in his works references to events and places that reflected English history and achievements. He also used familiar stories, including Greek myths and Roman history.

Shakespeare used the English language playfully, inventing puns and other figures of speech that we still use today, such as "tongue-tied," "high time," "seen better days," and "dead as a doornail." He also invented words like "hurry," "lonely," "excellent," "leapfrog," and almost two thousand others that we continue to use every day. In doing so he helped create a vigorous language that reflected England's rising status in the world.

Shakespeare knew that even serious dramas had to have a little humor. Other playwrights added slapstick comedy to make people laugh but which did not improve their plays. Shakespeare made sure that even his tragedies included humor, but he made it relevant to the plots. In the same way, his comedies were often thought-provoking too.

Finally, Shakespeare wrote with such insight into how people feel and behave that his characters seemed totally believable. He put the world on his stage and made people in his own time and ours laugh, cry, and think deeply. Because his plays are about the human qualities we all share, they transcended their times and still capture people's imaginations.

## THE IMMORTAL BARD

Shakespeare became one of the most popular dramatists in history; today his plays are performed in more languages and in more countries than those of any other playwright. They have been translated into almost one hundred languages. So much has been written about him and his works that the Folger Shakespeare Library in Washington, D.C., is crammed with thousands of books by or about him. His plays have inspired ballets, operas, musicals, and movies. Children study them at school, often unwillingly at first, because Shakespeare's language is no longer in use today and can be difficult to get used to. But he would have understood, since he wrote about unwilling schoolboys and even had been one himself.

Shakespeare would also be amused to know that a special word was invented to describe people's admiration for him: "bardolatry." It combines the word "bard," which means "storyteller," with the word "idolatry." Some people have reacted against the idolizing of Shakespeare, even arguing that he could not have written such great plays since he was only a commoner with a limited education. They have tried to claim that someone noble, or even royal—perhaps Queen Elizabeth I—must have written them. Serious historians laugh at these claims, though, because Shakespeare's life and fame are well documented.

While the language of Shakespeare may seem difficult to understand on the page, when performed it blossoms into life. Although our language has changed so much since his time, Shakespeare's understanding of human nature, his humor, and his way with words ensure that he will remain the Immortal Bard.

# SHAKESPEARE'S ENGLAND

SCOTLAND

Edinburgh

NORTH SEA

IRISH SEA

IRELAND

ENGLAND

WALES

Stratford-upon-Avon

London

ENGLISH CHANNEL

1. Shakespeare was born, raised, and married in Stratford-upon-Avon, eventually retiring there. He probably visited his family there only once a year while he lived in London.

2. Shakespeare was a boy when the English navy defeated the invading Spanish Armada. Such achievements probably contributed to his sense of England's destiny as a world leader.

3. It was in London that Shakespeare gained fame as an actor, playwright, and poet. Queen Elizabeth I was one of his fans.

4. When plague struck London in 1593, Shakespeare's actors toured the countryside.

5. Another great fan of Shakespeare was James I, King of England and Scotland, who succeeded Queen Elizabeth.

# Benjamin Franklin
*Colonial America, 1706–1790*

You probably know that Benjamin Franklin was one of the Founding Fathers of the United States, but did you know he was also a printer, author, public servant, inventor, scientist, and ambassador? His energy, wit, and optimism helped shape the new nation and the way its people saw themselves while his inventions and scientific discoveries made him just as well known and loved in Europe.

Ben Franklin was born in Boston, Massachusetts. With seventeen children, his parents could afford to send him to school for only two years. Then they apprenticed him to an older brother who ran a printing business. Ben continued his education by reading books, which were scarce in those days. Ben's brother treated him so harshly that he ran away at the age of seventeen. But in the next few years he would prosper. After working in England, he moved to Philadelphia, Pennsylvania, where he founded his own printing business and newspaper, married, and started a family.

There Franklin began publishing an almanac, which he called *Poor Richard's Almanack*, filled with astronomical tables, astrology, recipes, jokes, and proverbs like, "The early bird gets the worm." The *Almanack* made him famous throughout the American colonies. Only the Bible was more widely read.

Franklin believed that ordinary people working together could create the same benefits that were enjoyed by the nobility and the wealthy. He helped establish the first public library in North America, a police force, a volunteer fire department, a hospital, and an academy that became the University of Pennsylvania. Franklin even organized the first garbage collection service! Although roads were then merely dirt tracks, as postmaster of the colonies he made the postal service fast and reliable, giving the people a greater sense of community.

All his life, Franklin tried to improve the world around him. Among his inventions still in use today are a stove that emits more heat than a conventional fireplace, the lightning rod, bifocals, and the gliding rocking chair. He even invented a musical instrument called the armonica. Franklin never patented his inventions; they were for everyone's use. People all over the colonies and Europe were especially grateful for the stove and lightning rod, which made their homes warmer and safer.

Franklin was a shrewd but honest businessman, proud of his humble origins. When he was forty-two—an advanced age in those days—he retired from work to pursue his hobbies. He

learned French, Spanish, Italian, German, and Latin; worked for the colonial government; continued to invent things; and became interested in electricity.

At that time the science of electricity was a mystery, with no practical applications. Franklin devised various experiments to learn more about it. In one he proved that lightning was a form of electricity by flying a kite during a storm to draw off an electric charge from lightning. It is lucky he wasn't killed during this dangerous experiment! He invented words to describe his findings that are still in use today, like "battery," "conductor," and "plus and minus charges." His experiments made him famous as a scientist.

Always active in politics, Franklin was sent to England to represent the colonies in 1757. While crossing the Atlantic, he observed the Gulf Stream, a current that circulates around the ocean and can leave sailing ships motionless. He prompted the ship's captain to chart its movements to help navigators. In England Franklin spent many frustrating years lobbying lawmakers to persuade them to uphold colonial rights. Meanwhile, he made friends all over Europe, continued inventing and experimenting, and began an autobiography.

In 1775, realizing that England would never listen to the colonies' complaints, he returned home to support the American Revolution. He helped draft the Declaration of Independence and then sailed to France, where he urged the French to aid the revolutionaries. At the end of the Revolution, he helped negotiate peace with England and became the first U.S. ambassador to France.

*Settlers from Europe poured into North America looking for a new start in life. They saw the land as a vast wilderness waiting to be tamed by hard work.*

Home at last and failing in health, Franklin helped draft the new U.S. Constitution in the late 1780s. At his death, France actually held a larger funeral service for him than the Americans did. This multi-talented man had belonged not only to the United States but to the world.

## THE "NEW WORLD"

The British colonies in America offered opportunities to thousands of people. Displacing the Native

Americans, English, Scottish, Irish, Welsh, Dutch, and German settlers poured in from Europe. Some were looking for religious freedom, some wanted land. Others were merchants who imported products such as tea and cloth and exported animal pelts, salted fish, and tobacco.

Villages along the Atlantic coast grew into cities. Their streets were alternately muddy and dusty. Houses crowded together burned down before anyone could help. With unsanitary living conditions and little medical knowledge, epidemics of smallpox and other diseases hit repeatedly. Inland,

*Franklin enjoyed playing the plain-spoken rustic for the adoring French aristocracy.*

settlers built trading posts, farms, and forts. They confronted the elements, huge forests, wide rivers, disease, and unfriendly natives. They learned to make what they needed, from homespun clothing to horseshoes, or to do without. But always there was the promise of a prosperity denied to them in Europe.

As they became settled, the colonists realized they could produce and export their own goods. But English trading companies, protected by law, monopolized colonial trade. The British government profited from this system by taxing trade goods. There seemed to be more taxes all the time. In the 1760s, England defeated France in Canada after a long war, and she expected taxes from the colonies to pay for the victory.

When an English law or tax seemed unjust, colonists had difficulty getting Parliament to listen to their grievances. For example, wealthy nobles known as "proprietors" owned the colony of Pennsylvania. They lived luxuriously in England, indifferent to the hard life in America. The colonial governors worked for them. When taxes were raised for a militia to protect the colonists from Native American raiders, the nobles were exempted, even though they benefited. Those same nobles participated in Parliament and lobbied against the colonists, who had no representatives.

Such conflicts came to a boiling point in the late 1700s. When Benjamin Franklin went to England, he assumed that the colonists had the same rights as all Englishmen. He was confident that Parliament would listen, but instead he was met with hostility, arrogance, and indifference. Only when members of Parliament launched a vicious verbal attack on him did he recognize that his loyalty must now be to America.

## "SILENCE DOGOOD" AND OTHER CHARACTERS

Benjamin Franklin helped mold the character of the colonies with the "characters" he created during his life. While apprenticed to his older brother, he wanted to contribute to his brother's newspaper. Knowing his brother would not take him seriously, Ben invented a character, "Silence Dogood," who could do his speaking for him. After work he left "her" letters at the print shop, where his brother found and printed them. Poking fun at Bostonians' prejudices and championing ideals such as freedom of speech and education for women, they were an instant success.

Years later Franklin invented another character for his almanac—"Poor Richard"—who humorously reported on his life. He was also the mouthpiece for Franklin's thoughts on freedom, justice, and public spirit. These ideas helped shape his fellow colonists' attitudes and paved the way for the foundation of a democracy after the American Revolution.

Even later, as an old man Franklin himself became a character when he arrived in France to promote the American Revolution. He was greeted by adoring crowds. They wanted to see the great scientist who had tamed lightning. Dressed for his journey in simple dark clothing and a beaver-skin hat, he became an instant fashion sensation. Franklin actually liked to dress elegantly, but when he saw the impact his traveling clothes made on the French, he played his new role willingly. He continued to dress simply, creating an image of the new American, earthy and plain-speaking.

Benjamin Franklin played many roles as he continued to learn from life's experiences. As he aged he was able to drop many of the prejudices of his time. He came to realize the evils of slavery and the hypocrisy of white mistreatment of "primitive" natives.

Franklin became the model of the self-made man who worked hard and honestly to improve his own life and that of others. His humor, talent, and vision made him a true Founding Father. At the end of his life he wrote, "God grant that not only the love of liberty, but a thorough knowledge of the rights of man, may pervade all the nations of the earth, so that a philosopher may set his foot anywhere on its surface, and say, 'This is my country.'"

# BENJAMIN FRANKLIN'S WORLD

1. Benjamin Franklin was born in Boston, where he learned the printing business from his brother.

2. Franklin ran away to Philadelphia, returning there after spending some time in England. In Philadelphia he eventually became a successful printer and also a prominent citizen and scientist.

3. Franklin sailed to England again, this time as a well-known man. He observed the course of the Gulf Stream and had the ship's captain map it out for him.

4. During the years leading up to the American Revolution, Franklin represented colonial interests in London.

5. Benjamin Franklin also served as the first U.S. ambassador to France.

# Wolfgang Amadeus Mozart

*Austria, 1756–1791*

Have you ever sung "Twinkle, Twinkle, Little Star"? Did you know that Wolfgang Amadeus Mozart probably wrote it when he was only five years old? Both his father Leopold and his older sister Nannerl were talented musicians, but neither of them could match little Wolfgang. By the age of five he had mastered the piano and violin and was writing his own music.

Mozart's father decided to profit from his children's talents. In eighteenth-century Europe musicians and composers were supported by the wealthy ruling classes. He was sure that rulers and nobles all over Europe would love these musical child prodigies and shower them with money and other gifts. Leopold set off with Nannerl and Wolfgang on a series of performing tours across Europe. In those days, fathers had absolute control over their families, and no one thought it odd for Leopold to put his children to work. He was proud of them.

Everywhere they went, the children delighted audiences. They performed for kings, queens, nobles, and churchmen, and indeed received gifts of money, clothes, wigs, a little sword for Wolfgang, watches, and musical boxes. But they had to work long hours, and both fell seriously ill several times. Still, they loved seeing the world, and Wolfgang met other fine musicians who taught him even more about music.

As Mozart grew up, he began to look for his own wealthy patrons. But despite his talent, he never seemed to find a suitable position. One reason was that jealous rivals plotted against him behind his back. Another was Mozart's own independent spirit. He wanted respect for himself and his music, and was reluctant to play only what someone else wanted to hear.

By his mid-twenties, Mozart realized that he would not find a permanent patron. He now had a wife and children to support. He tried making a living by teaching music, giving public performances, accepting commissions, and selling his compositions. He also wrote music for his own pleasure.

No matter how hard he worked and how much money he made, Mozart fell into increasing debt. He was never good at budgeting his money. After his childhood illnesses, he was not very strong either. His constant work and concern about money took their toll. At the age of thirty-five, he fell mortally ill, possibly from kidney disease, but he continued to compose even as he lay dying.

Mozart's widow, Constanze, kept his reputation alive, and her second husband wrote Mozart's first biography. Over time more and more of his music came to light. No other composer has produced so many kinds of music, and few have written as much as he did—almost 650 complete pieces. He even wrote a piece for Benjamin Franklin's armonica.

Mozart knew he was leaving a gift to the world through his music. Today he is more popular than ever.

## MOZART'S EUROPE

On their tours the young Mozarts grew accustomed to special treatment, since even kings and queens received them so graciously. Once little Wolfgang jumped into the lap of the Austrian empress and gave her a kiss. Luckily, she was amused. Like most rulers then, she held absolute power and could have had him punished severely since he was only a servant.

*To entertain noble patrons while he was on tour, little Wolfgang even performed blindfolded sometimes.*

Although the Mozarts worked for the wealthy nobility, they never thought of themselves as servants. They had friends from many social levels. However, some of their rivals wanted only to climb the social scale; they snubbed those below them and betrayed those around them.

As charming young children, Wolfgang and Nannerl threatened no one in this competitive world. But when they were grown, they were no longer considered cute and unthreatening. Nannerl stopped traveling and began teaching music at home. Because he was small and looked young for his age, Wolfgang was able to tour longer, but eventually he had to look for work under a wealthy patron. Even though he was admired universally, sometimes rival musicians tried to sabotage him. His extreme pride got in his way too.

The rich people Mozart had to please did not like his independent ways. They expected him to entertain them humbly or to glorify them. Once one of Mozart's employers took him on a trip to another city. Mozart hated eating with the servants and waiting for hours in case his patron might want a little music. The man also paid Mozart poorly but refused to let him earn extra money by composing for anyone else. Mozart finally left in a rage and vowed to make a living independently.

Mozart's desire to earn a living on his own was revolutionary for a musician in his day. He was not the only person with new and different ideas, though. During his lifetime, two major political upheavals would shape a new Europe: the American and French revolutions. Both uprisings came about because common people felt they were being treated unfairly. People across Europe began to question the enormous power held by the monarchs and the nobility. Eventually, the system that Mozart found so suffocating began to break down.

Mozart hinted at how people of the "lower" classes felt in one of his funniest operas, *The Marriage of Figaro*, in which the masters are silly and incompetent while the servants are clever and capable. Operas in his time functioned the way films and television do today: they entertained and spread ideas. Mozart was no firebrand ready to overthrow the government, but he did poke fun at the type of people who could not appreciate his genius.

## FOR THE LOVE OF MUSIC

Mozart learned to read and write music before he could read and write words. By the time he was eight, he had composed a symphony. By the time he was twelve, he had written his first opera.

Mozart enjoyed writing music even more than performing it. When he created music in later years, he finished it in his head before he ever wrote it down. He knew exactly where he wanted horns or violins or clarinets to play. Sometimes he had

*Operas like* The Magic Flute *combined music, spectacle, fantasy, and perhaps a secret message. Was the Queen of the Night a veiled caricature of the Empress of Austria, whom he had once kissed and now regarded as a tyrant?*

to add paper to his music sheets to make room for instructions for each of the different instruments. He rarely made changes after he wrote a piece, and he could write anywhere or at any time. Mozart wrote while talking with friends, playing billiards, and even holding his wife's hand while she was having a baby! He worked late every night, sometimes finishing music only hours before it was to be performed.

Mozart wrote symphonies, operas, church music, and both light and serious compositions. He hoped that everyone would enjoy his work, and most did. People hummed his tunes as they walked down the streets, just like we do today with our favorite songs. However, because there were no copyright or royalty laws, even Mozart's popular music did not keep making money for him. Unlike today's composers, who are paid each time a piece is played, he was paid only once for each work no matter how often it was performed, so he had to continue composing and looking for commissions.

Mozart had to pay another price for his independence also. He was constantly in debt because he had to keep up appearances to attract more business. This meant paying for servants, nice clothes, an attractive apartment, and entertainment for wealthy friends. Because of this the Mozarts had to do without other things. Once a friend dropped by and found Wolfgang and Constanze whirling about their parlor. He thought they were dancing, but Mozart confided that they were trying to keep warm since they could not afford more wood for the fire.

As he neared the end of his life, Mozart received a commission from a mysterious visitor who wanted him to write a requiem—music for a funeral. The stranger refused to identify himself. He was actually just an agent for someone who bought other people's music to pass off as his own. But Mozart, whose health was failing, became convinced that the requiem would be for his own funeral. Mozart began to write feverishly—some of his greatest compositions—as though he knew he was running out of time. Then he fell deathly ill. He struggled desperately to finish the requiem, even dictating it to a friend when he grew too weak to write, but he did not live to complete it.

Had he lived, Mozart probably would have become financially successful eventually. He knew that one day his genius would be recognized. We might feel sad that he died so young, but he faced death with confidence. For him death was part of life, and his life was happy because he spent it doing what he loved.

# MOZART TOURS EUROPE

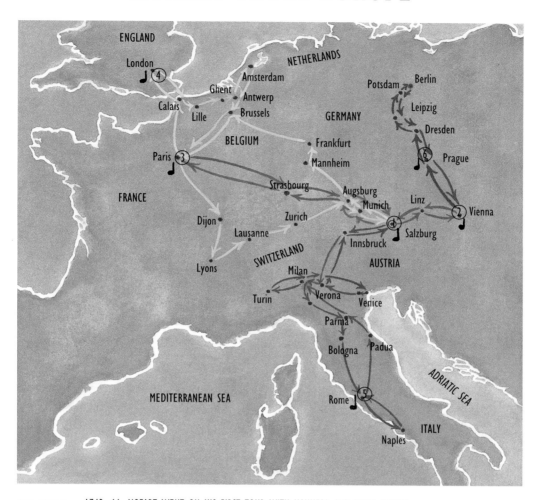

| | |
|---|---|
| | 1763–66 MOZART WENT ON HIS FIRST TOUR WITH NANNERL AND THEIR FATHER. |
| | 1770 MOZART TOURED AGAIN WITH HIS FATHER; HIS FUTURE SEEMED ASSURED. |
| | 1777–78 MOZART TOURED WITH HIS MOTHER. |
| | 1789–90 MOZART'S LAST TOUR IN AN ATTEMPT TO GET OUT OF DEBT. |

1. Mozart was born and raised in Salzburg, Austria, but his father took him and his sister all over Europe. Throughout his life, he performed and composed wherever he went.

2. On their first visit to Vienna, the young Mozarts performed for the Empress of Austria. As an adult, Wolfgang and his wife, Constanze, moved to Vienna, where he died in 1791.

3. Mozart made two trips to Paris: on the first, he entertained the king and queen; on the second, he toured with his mother, trying to find patrons.

4. In London, the Mozarts were welcomed on their first tour. As an adult, Mozart was invited back and, had he lived, he might have found security there.

5. Mozart's second hugely successful tour was to Italy. In Rome, the Pope awarded him the order of the golden spur, a major honor.

6. In Prague (then part of Bohemia), Mozart was adored for his music. At the request of the city, he wrote a symphony (No. 38, the *Prague)* and an opera (*Don Giovanni*), some of his best music.

# Sequoyah

*United States, circa 1770–1843*

Around 1770 a Native American Cherokee boy was born in what is now the state of Tennessee. His name was Sequoyah, "the Lame One." Although he always walked with a limp, Sequoyah did not let this stop him from achieving his vision. He helped his people through one of the darkest times in their history by giving them the gift of writing.

When Sequoyah grew up, he designed silver jewelry for his fellow Cherokees, made shoes for their horses, and ran a trading post. He and his wife and children also farmed and raised livestock, customs they had adopted from the white settlers who were moving in around the Cherokees. Many of these settlers cut down forests, ploughed the land, killed or drove away the wild animals that the Cherokees hunted for food, and brought new diseases that would kill the native peoples who had no resistance to them.

All around the once-vast Cherokee nation, whites were demanding that the tribes give them land. They wanted the natives to move farther west, where whites had not yet settled. Some Cherokees had done just that, and now there was an eastern and a western branch of their nation. They hardly ever heard from one another unless a traveler brought news.

Sequoyah's contacts with white people introduced him to books and writing. He observed that, with these "talking leaves" (written pages), people could convey wisdom and speak to each other across distances. Sequoyah's people had always used their rich store of tales, rituals, symbols, and memory devices such as wampum belts to pass on their heritage, but times were changing. He decided that his people needed talking leaves too to help the eastern and western Cherokees reunite and save their traditional teachings.

Without ever learning to read or speak English, Sequoyah spent twelve years developing a Cherokee writing system. He borrowed symbols from the whites' alphabet and then added some that he invented. He first thought to make each symbol represent a different word, but that was too complicated. So he developed a simpler approach whereby each symbol represented a different syllable. His system had eighty-six symbols and was completely phonetic, without any complex spelling rules. It also represented the actual sounds of the Cherokee language, which the white alphabet did not.

During these years, Sequoyah's fellow Cherokees ridiculed him for his efforts. Some thought he was crazy. But in 1821 he persuaded the Cherokee National Council to watch a demonstration as his six-year-old daughter read aloud from a letter she had never seen

before. Within a few hours Sequoyah had also taught several young men to read. The chiefs immediately realized the value of his "syllabary." They launched a campaign to spread Cherokee writing. It was so easy to learn that people could teach others immediately after they had learned it. A whole nation became literate within months.

Using Sequoyah's invention, the chiefs then began a campaign to preserve Cherokee rights to their homelands. In 1828 Sequoyah helped the chiefs draw up a Cherokee constitution written in Cherokee syllabary and modeled on the U.S. Constitution. That same year a Cherokee newspaper using his syllabary began publication. Sequoyah also represented his people in Washington, D.C. Around this time, he was moved to Arkansas territory, where he taught many western Cherokees to read and write.

*To drive off their Cherokee neighbors, white settlers often attacked and burned Cherokee homes.*

However, the efforts of the Cherokees to preserve their nation could not hold back the tide of white settlers. In 1838 the Cherokees were forcibly removed from their homelands and resettled on a reservation far to the west. Sequoyah did not give up, however. Until his disappearance in Mexico in 1843, he continued to travel among his people, teaching them to read and write. They used their new writing skills to stay in touch with each other and to begin rebuilding their lives.

Although the Cherokee syllabary is no longer in use, Sequoyah's name did find immortality. The giant California sequoia trees, among the largest and oldest living things on earth, bear his name, a tribute to his vision of a strong and lasting Cherokee people.

## A UNITED NATION

When Europeans arrived in North America, they regarded the Native Americans as primitive savages. They thought their own religion, ideas, and modern tools (like guns, ploughs, wheels, writing, and money) made them more civilized. And they hungered for land in a way that the natives could not understand.

After the American Revolution, European immigrants poured into North America looking for a better life. To them wealth meant good farmland. The settlers who moved into native homelands believed they had a right to use these fertile areas for farming. In their view the land was going to waste, and surely there was plenty for all.

What the whites did not realize was that the Native American way of life depended on a different use of the land. The Cherokees occupied the beautiful mountain regions of what is now the southeastern United States. They hunted large animals that needed space to roam. They also farmed and gathered roots, berries, and medicinal plants widely scattered in the forests. They cherished their land, the resting place of their beloved ancestors. The idea of owning a little plot of it seemed silly and destructive to them as they believed no one could own land. They believed that land belonged equally to everyone to use with care. White settlers thus were destroying both the balance of nature and traditional native life.

*Wealthy, northern-educated, and blue-eyed, John Ross was only one-eighth Cherokee, but he was totally devoted to his tribe.*

In addition, the new U.S. government—and dishonest individuals—made treaties promising to pay for native land that was taken and not to seize any more. But the payments were not made, and the treaties were always broken, especially after gold was discovered in some areas.

As they were slowly pushed off their lands, the Cherokees fought back. They formed themselves into a nation led by their visionary chief John Ross. Ross aroused tremendous public support for his people in the northern states, but not enough to counter the hostility to Native Americans in the South.

The united Cherokees fought a long legal battle against the white invaders. They used the U.S. courts, the press, hard bargaining, and nonviolent resistance in their struggle to stay on their homelands and to remain a nation. In 1829 one lawsuit even reached the U.S. Supreme Court, which decided in their favor. But President Andrew Jackson refused to enforce the decision.

By then Sequoyah had moved west, but he followed the Cherokees' struggle to keep their homes. More and more of their lands were organized into new states. The final blow came when gold was discovered in Cherokee territory. The United States wanted it, and eventually the Cherokees and other tribes were ordered to leave their lands and move west.

Most Cherokees refused. They hid in the forests and mountains. Whites burned their villages and seized their belongings, but they still held out, peaceably refusing to fight back. Finally, in 1838 thousands were rounded up in surprise raids. Their homes and even the graves of their ancestors were looted while they were marched off, forced to leave everything behind. Over a quarter of the tribe died of disease, cold, and starvation as they were driven west along what is still called the "Trail of Tears."

Resettled in what was designated "Indian Territory," the Cherokees rebuilt their lives and worked out their differences with other displaced tribes, some of them old enemies. They also survived the U.S. Civil War and further invasions by white people. Eventually, the Cherokee nation had to dissolve when "Indian Territory" became the state of Oklahoma in 1907. However, the first congressional representatives from the new state were Cherokee, a sign of the tribe's lasting strength and vitality. Yet given a choice, they would have named the new state Sequoyah.

## A MAN WITH A VISION

Sequoyah may not have appreciated just how unique his achievement was. Never before nor since has one person invented a writing system for a whole people. It usually takes centuries of trial and error for writing to develop. Sequoyah did realize that his invention could help other tribes. In his old age he traveled and taught his syllabary to them as well.

We can imagine Sequoyah outside someone's home, surrounded by children and their parents. He uses a stick to trace syllables in the dirt and pronounces each one carefully. Soon the whole group is practicing. Some use knives or charcoal to trace the symbols on pieces of bark. Excitedly, they practice writing and reading to each other. After a day or so, Sequoyah goes to another settlement, hoping that his writing system will help the native peoples preserve their great traditions.

# SEQUOYAH'S AMERICA

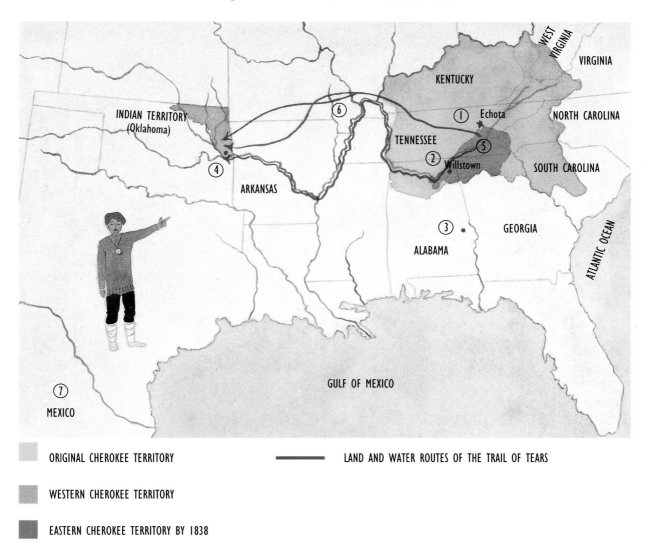

ORIGINAL CHEROKEE TERRITORY — LAND AND WATER ROUTES OF THE TRAIL OF TEARS

WESTERN CHEROKEE TERRITORY

EASTERN CHEROKEE TERRITORY BY 1838

1. Sequoyah was born near the old Cherokee capital of Echota.

2. As a young man, Sequoyah lived in Willstown, working as a silversmith and blacksmith until he moved to Arkansas. He returned to Willstown to demonstrate his syllabary.

3. As allies of the U.S., Sequoyah and his fellow warriors helped defeat the Creek tribe at the Battle of Horseshoe Bend. They were led by Andrew Jackson, who later, as president, did not intervene when the state of Georgia forcibly removed the Cherokees.

4. In 1818, Sequoyah joined the western Cherokees in Arkansas, continuing to work on his syllabary. He returned there after demonstrating his syllabary to the National Council in 1821.

5. In 1838, about 5,000 Cherokees were rounded up and imprisoned in stockades, where they began to die even before being marched off.

6. John Ross persuaded the U.S. to let the remaining Cherokees organize their own departure, and 13,000 more made the long journey west, during which over a quarter died, including Ross's wife.

7. In 1842, Sequoyah journeyed to Mexico to find more Cherokees rumored to have settled there. It was there that he died.

# Mohandas Gandhi,
# the "Mahatma"

*India, 1869–1948*

To millions of Indians, Mohandas Gandhi was the Mahatma, the "Great Soul." Believing that truth and nonviolent resistance could be a more effective means of change than weapons, Gandhi helped India attain independence from Great Britain without a bloody revolution.

Shy and sensitive, Gandhi grew up in a traditional Hindu family, where he learned respect for all living things. He also had a stubborn streak that led him to make his own decisions. Breaking with tradition, he left his young wife, Kasturbai, in India and went to England to study law. There he discovered and developed a passion for the idea of justice.

Back in India, Gandhi was too shy to be a successful lawyer. He finally found work in South Africa, where nonwhite people such as Indians were considered inferior and often very badly treated. Soon after he and his family arrived, he was thrown off a train by whites because of his dark skin. Gandhi was so outraged that he vowed to overcome his shyness to speak out against and change the situation. He believed that all citizens of the British empire should be treated as equals.

Gandhi decided to use as his weapons what are known in Sanskrit as *satyagraha* (the force of truth) and *ahimsa* (nonharm to others). He would lead strikes, make speeches, and work for justice, but he would never use violence. He would oppose the hatred and violence of those who oppressed others, confident that they would eventually accept truth and justice. In South Africa he plunged into local politics, founded a newspaper, set up retreat centers where people could learn about satyagraha, and led peaceful protest marches. Kasturbai loyally helped him.

Gandhi's successful campaigns for the rights of Indians in South Africa made him famous in India and England. He returned to India in the early 1900s, already a trusted leader. He wanted to reform certain aspects of Indian life that he felt weakened the country, including raising the status of millions of impoverished peasants and overcoming hatred between Muslims and Hindus.

Gandhi wanted to reform India as a step toward achieving his greatest goal, Indian independence from Great Britain. After his experiences in South Africa, he no longer believed that the empire could benefit Indians. He saw that Britain wanted to keep India

both politically and economically dependent. For instance, Indians had once woven their own cloth. Now they were expected to buy mass-produced English cloth instead. Wherever Gandhi went, he taught villagers how to spin so they could produce their own cloth. Spinning came to symbolize India's drive for independence.

Just as he had done in Africa, Gandhi founded several ashrams, or religious retreat centers, where people could study satyagraha, and then went home to organize nonviolent resistance to British rule.

For almost forty years Gandhi and his followers campaigned for India's freedom. He led nonviolent strikes and marches, fasted, and prayed. Repeatedly imprisoned and nearly dying from his fasts, he worked tirelessly to promote freedom and self-reliance for all Indians.

In 1948 India achieved independence, but at a price. Even Gandhi could not bridge the gulf between Hindus and Muslims. As religious violence exploded, the British government partitioned India into two countries, Hindu India and Muslim Pakistan, thinking this step would prevent civil war. Instead millions of Hindus and Muslims found themselves on the wrong side of the new borders. Fighting broke out on both sides. Gandhi was aghast and, in an attempt to stop the bloodshed, fasted so rigorously that he nearly died. This did indeed help stop some of the fighting, as most Indians adored him and wanted him to live. However, Hindu extremists blamed Gandhi for the partition, and one of them assassinated him. Indians were devastated, and people around the world mourned.

## THE INDIAN EMPIRE

India is so large that it is called a subcontinent. It stretches across towering mountains, steamy jungles, and dusty plains. It supports millions of people whose culture is ancient, rich, and varied. It is home to a unique national religion, Hinduism.

India was invaded by Muslim conquerors in the

*India's ancient, rich, and varied culture seemed exotic and glamorous to the English.*

58

thirteenth century. Their descendants ruled many areas of India up to the twentieth century. By then the British had taken control, first through trade, then through military might.

India became the "jewel in the crown" of the British empire. England brought over governors and educators, built an enormous railway system, and educated some upper-caste Indians in England, all in the interest of controlling India's vast wealth. Half of India's revenues went back to England, while the peasants suffered from starvation and the lack of education and medical care. In addition the British divided Indians against each other, often favoring Muslims over Hindus.

According to Hindu tradition, each person is born into a hereditary social rank, or caste: priest, warrior, tradesman, or laborer. At the lowest level of society were the "outcastes," or "untouchables." They could only do the work that no one else wanted. They lacked education, health care, and decent living conditions. The English saw the existence of the caste system as proof of Indian inferiority.

Indians entered the twentieth century ready for change. They wanted independence, and they wanted to decide for themselves what their country should be like. Gandhi became a focus for India's desire for independence and self-esteem.

Gandhi understood that some aspects of Indian culture did indeed present a

*As was traditional, Kasturbai did not meet Gandhi before they married. Less traditionally though, she participated in politics and social reform due to her loyalty to Gandhi.*

problem. For instance, as long as outcastes were treated badly by their own people, the English were bound to feel that they had a right to rule and educate the Indian nation in the English style. Calling the outcastes harijans, or "God's children," Gandhi worked to raise their status.

## THE SALT MARCH

One way the British controlled Indians was through monopolizing the production and sale of salt. In a hot country like India, a lack of salt in the diet can be fatal. Paying for it was a hardship for the poor, even though India had more than enough salt on its beaches and in its seas.

Gandhi chose this issue to highlight the unfairness of the British system. In 1930 he decided to walk to the sea from his ashram at Ahmedabad, a distance of almost 250 miles, and to make his own salt from seawater. He announced his plans to the press and began his march with a few followers. Newspapers and radios around the world carried the story of his journey. As word spread more and more people joined him. By the time he reached the sea at Dandi, twenty-four days later, thousands of people had joined his march.

When Gandhi and his followers began making salt from seawater, they broke the British monopoly. Up and down the coastline of India, people began making their own salt. The salt they collected was not very good, but this project proved they could work together peaceably to oppose the British. More nonviolent protests followed. Over sixty thousand people were arrested, but their determination and willingness to sacrifice themselves finally wore down the British. They repealed the salt laws.

It takes a special kind of greatness to inspire people to risk their lives for a cause, especially when they commit themselves to nonviolence. Gandhi's uncompromising gentleness made a deep impression on both the English and the Indians as well as others. Wherever he went, people flocked to him for advice and blessings. To the Indian people, he was not just a politician—he was a saint.

NEW BOUNDARIES OF DIVIDED EMPIRE

1. Mohandas Gandhi was born in Porbandar in 1869.

2. Gandhi grew up in Rajkot and was married to Kasturbai there when they were thirteen.

3. After studying law in London, Gandhi worked in Bombay. Too shy to try cases, he got a job in South Africa in 1898.

4. Most Indians in South Africa worked on plantations as near-slaves. After being dumped off a train by whites between Durban and Pretoria, Gandhi became determined to defend Indian rights without violence. He also founded an ashram called Tolstoy Farm, after the Russian author and pacifist.

5. In 1916, now famous for his work in South Africa, Gandhi returned home and began touring and teaching throughout India. He founded several ashrams, including one at Ahmedabad, from which his Salt March began in 1930.

6. Gandhi and Kasturbai lived in another ashram at Nagpur from 1935 to 1945.

7. Often imprisoned (Kasturbai by his side), such as at Pune, Gandhi still influenced Indians by fasting nearly to death.

8. In 1947, after the partition of India into India and Pakistan, Gandhi quelled riots in Calcutta by fasting.

9. Gandhi did the same in Delhi in early 1948, shaming both Hindus and Muslims into calling a truce. However, he was shot and killed by a Hindu extremist there who blamed him for the break-up of India.

# BRITAIN'S INDIAN EMPIRE

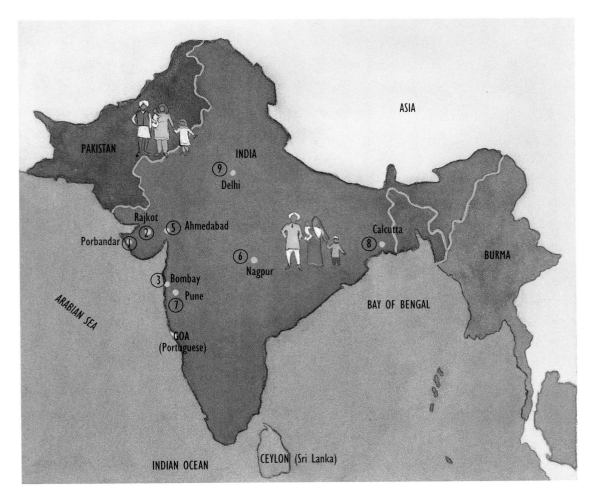

ASIA

PAKISTAN

INDIA

⑨ Delhi

Rajkot

② ⑤ Ahmedabad

Porbandar ①

⑥ Nagpur

Calcutta

⑧

BURMA

③ Bombay

⑦ Pune

ARABIAN SEA

BAY OF BENGAL

GOA
(Portuguese)

INDIAN OCEAN

CEYLON (Sri Lanka)

# SOUTH AFRICAN COLONIES

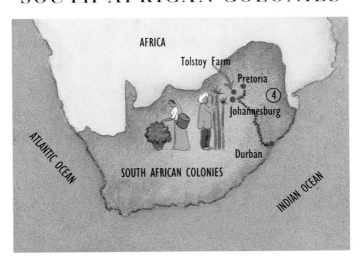

AFRICA

Tolstoy Farm

Pretoria

④

Johannesburg

Durban

SOUTH AFRICAN COLONIES

ATLANTIC OCEAN

INDIAN OCEAN

# Albert Einstein

*Germany/United States, 1879–1955*

As Albert Einstein was growing up in Germany, he found everything around him to be both wondrous and puzzling. When he was twelve, he decided to set about solving what he called "the riddle of the huge world." In his quest for an answer, Einstein revolutionized modern science.

Einstein decided that physics might offer him some understanding of the world. (Physics is the study of space, time, matter, and energy—everything from the tiniest atomic particles to the greatest galaxies.) After completing his university studies, he worked as an office clerk by day and on his own ideas at night. In 1905, when he was twenty-six, Einstein began publishing scientific papers explaining his new theories. Some scientists scoffed at his ideas, especially when they found out he was not a university professor. Other scientists were intrigued and tested Einstein's hypotheses for themselves. Their observations confirmed what his theories predicted.

Before Einstein developed his theories, people had thought space was like a huge, empty container and that time passed even if nothing was happening. They thought that the universe moved separately inside space and time. But there were many things this view could not explain. Einstein proposed that time, space, and matter are all related. Without matter in the universe, both space and time could not exist. Einstein added that light is bent by gravity, that space is curved, and that time appears to move more slowly for objects that move faster.

Most people felt that Einstein's new theories could only be understood by fellow scientists, but today many people at least know his famous formula, $E = mc^2$. It relates matter, energy, and light to one another. Einstein said that what we see as solid objects are in fact condensed energy. To find an object's energy, multiply the speed of light first by itself and then by the mass of the object. Therefore, E (energy) = m (mass) x $c^2$ (speed of light x itself). Based on his theories, scientists figured out how to split atoms, which is how nuclear power is created.

Einstein won the Nobel Prize for science in 1921. He also became a scientific superstar, adored all over the world, which embarrassed him. He spent the rest of his life searching for a simple law of the universe that could unite all scientific laws.

At the same time Einstein and his discoveries were swept into world politics. In 1914 Germany had plunged into World War I. But believing in the unity of humankind, Einstein openly opposed this and all war. He was convinced it only harmed and divided people. Then,

in the 1920s and 1930s, the Nazi Party rose to power in Germany. One of its goals was to wipe out what it called the "inferior races," and Jews were its special target, among others. Although he did not practice Judaism, Einstein was born Jewish and became an object of particular hatred to the Nazis. Unable to withstand their attacks, he moved to the United States, taking a position as a professor at Princeton University in New Jersey.

During World War II, Einstein heard that the Nazis were developing atomic weapons based on his discoveries. He wrote to the president of the United States to warn him. But in fact it was the Americans who developed atomic bombs first and who used them to end World War II, causing horrifying destruction. Einstein had not intended his discoveries for such uses and regretted his part in their creation. Feeling that "we have won the war, but we have not won the peace," he spent the rest of his life working not only for science but for world peace.

*As a boy, Einstein loved to walk in the country, taking in the mystery and wonder of nature.*

## A WORLD DIVIDED

Throughout Europe's history, Jews have been persecuted. When the Nazi leader Adolf Hitler came to power in Germany, he made the Jewish people into scapegoats for all Germany's ills. He encouraged people to hate and fear Jews, claiming they were of a different, inferior race from other Europeans. He tried to discredit Einstein and his "Jewish" theories, even though Nazi scientists used them in their own war research. Hitler claimed that Germans were a pure "master race" destined to rule the world. He wanted to kill off not only the Jews but the other so-called inferior races. His list included gypsies, Catholics, and anyone who opposed him.

As German persecution increased, Einstein came to believe that Jews must leave Europe and reestablish their ancient homeland in Palestine in the Middle East. They had been exiled from Palestine by the

Romans two thousand years earlier. Many had moved back and built settlements, but Palestine, under Turkish rule until 1918, was now under British mandate.

Hitler's dictates triggered World War II, and thousands of Jews fled Europe. In the United States, Einstein used his influence to help these refugees. After the war the world learned that Hitler's Nazis had murdered millions of people, including more than six million Jews.

The Allies who had fought against Hitler agreed that the Jews must be given back their ancient homeland as a way to heal the deep wounds caused by the war and to provide a secure base for them. The new Jewish state of Israel was founded in 1948 in the land of Palestine. The first prime minister, David Ben-Gurion, asked Einstein to come to Israel to be its president. Although he felt honored, Einstein refused; he was a scientist, not a politician.

Unfortunately, Einstein's dream of a Jewish nation met with many obstacles. Israel was founded against the wishes of the Arab people already living in Palestine. War erupted again, this time between the new Israeli state and its neighbors. Einstein passed away while this conflict continued, still hoping for a world where people could realize they are all related, just as matter and energy are.

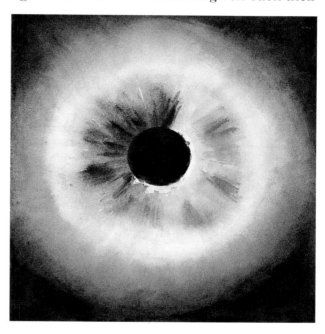

*In 1919, English scientists tested Einstein's theory of relativity by observing a total solar eclipse in Africa and Brazil. This proved Einstein's prediction that starlight is bent by the sun's gravity!*

## EINSTEIN'S IMAGINATION

Nowadays, when we call someone a genius we often say the person is an "Einstein." However, Albert Einstein often got poor grades as a result of the strict, regimented teaching he received that did not allow for his creativity. One of his teachers said he would never amount to anything. They did not understand his creative imagination, which he used in all his studies. When he was sixteen, he dreamed of riding on a beam of light. That experience gave him his first insight into relativity and led him to study physics at the university.

After leaving the university, Einstein continued to study and think about physics. While observing something, he imagined what it would do under different conditions. Then he worked out his theories mathematically and made predictions about how things should work if those theories were true. For instance, traditionally the word "mass" had been used in two different ways. One kind of mass (inertial mass) results in resistance when objects are pushed. Another type of mass (gravitational mass) is defined as the gravitational force between two bodies. With his theory of relativity, Einstein stated that both kinds of mass are the same. He maintained that, if this is true, the two aspects of mass would cancel each other out in a falling object. Thus people falling from a great height would feel weightless. You can test this part of his theory for yourself when you ride a roller coaster.

Einstein also stated that there is no such thing as absolute time. He suggested instead that time is experienced differently for objects moving relative to one another. For instance, people flying in a spaceship feel that the ship is standing still while the earth is moving away. But people on earth feel that the ship is moving away while the earth is standing still. To someone on earth the clocks on the ship would seem to move more slowly than those on earth, while to someone on the ship the clocks on earth would seem to move more slowly. It would be no good asking which time is the true time!

Einstein changed the way we see our world. Yet he had trouble accepting the changes his theories brought about. Other scientists used them not only to invent atomic weapons but also to explore the unpredictable, indeterminate qualities of our world. Einstein intensely disliked their ideas, and found himself more and more isolated from new scientific developments. However, he continued to attract world attention as he tried to discover a new unifying law of the universe. Einstein died without finding such a law, but he did alter the entire direction of modern physics. Inspired by his example, scientists are still trying to solve "the riddle of the huge world."

# EINSTEIN IN EUROPE

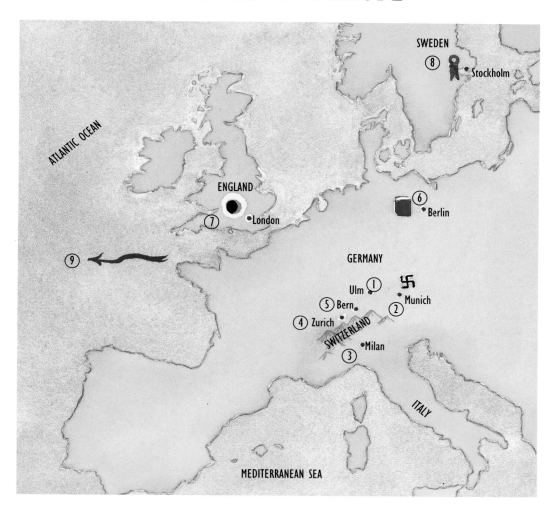

1. Albert Einstein was born in 1879, in the little town of Ulm, Germany.

2. When Einstein was a baby, his family moved to Munich, Germany, where he grew up.

3. Einstein dropped out of school and followed his family to Milan, Italy, when he was fifteen.

4. Soon he was back at school, in Zurich, Switzerland. Graduating from university in 1900, he became a Swiss citizen.

5. Unable to get a university professorship, he worked in the Swiss Patent Office in Bern, continued studying on his own, and published his theories in scientific journals.

6. By 1914, Einstein was already respected in the scientific community and had become a university professor. He settled in Berlin, where he witnessed Germany enthusiastically plunging into war.

7. In 1919, the Royal Society in London announced its findings from a solar eclipse in Africa and Brazil, thereby proving Einstein's theory of relativity to be correct. He became famous overnight, and began traveling and teaching around the world.

8. Einstein received the Nobel Prize at Stockholm in 1921, but in pre-Nazi Germany he found himself increasingly under suspicion as an outspoken pacifist and a Jew.

9. By 1933, he finally had to leave Germany, accepting a position at Princeton University in the United States. In 1939, he wrote to President Roosevelt, warning him that Nazi Germany might be developing nuclear weapons, and he died in Princeton in 1955.

# Jorge Luis Borges

*Argentina, 1899–1986*

*"Dreaming is my task . . . I am astonished at things"*

Born in Buenos Aires, Argentina, Jorge Luis Borges belonged to two worlds. One was the land and culture of Argentina: great mountains and plains, rivers, jungles, and deserts; gauchos (Argentine cowboys); the tango (a dance); and revolutionary patriotism. The other was the world of books and dreams. In his writing Borges merged the two to become one of the greatest Spanish-language authors of the twentieth century.

As a boy, Borges was short, shy, and nearsighted. His famous ancestors had fought for Argentine freedom, but he was a target for bullies. He could not fight like they did, so he read and wrote about imaginary worlds. There his physical weakness did not count.

Borges's family moved to Europe when he was a teenager. They were in Switzerland when World War I erupted and had to stay there until it ended. Reading on his own, Borges discovered myths, adventures, and mysteries from around the world. They echoed his feeling that life is mysterious and sometimes frightening, but always magical. After the war, Borges and his family traveled to Spain, where he became friends with other young writers. They hated the long-winded, stylized writing that was popular at the time and wanted to create a bolder, simpler Spanish literature. Borges had a flair for writing in this new way.

When his family returned to Buenos Aires in 1921, Borges introduced this new literary movement to Argentina. He wrote poems, essays, and short stories, edited magazines and books, and translated famous works of literature into Spanish. His readers enjoyed his gentle wit and wide-ranging imagination.

However, Borges's eyesight was beginning to fail. In 1938, he had struck his head against the corner of an open casement window. The wound became infected, and he nearly died. He was unable to speak for a while and was terrified he would not be able to write again. When he recovered from this injury, Borges began to write in a style that combined realism, science fiction, fantasy, and history. Some stories were funny and others were eerie, but they always blurred the line between dreaming and waking, fantasy and reality. This style became popular throughout Latin America and is now referred to as "magic realism."

Borges's income from writing could not support him, and he was too shy to lecture or teach as other authors did. Instead, despite his increasing blindness, he worked in a library.

69

There his fellow workers did not know about his writing career. They did not even recognize him when they saw an article about him in an encyclopedia.

Wider fame came to Borges in the 1940s with the rise of the powerful dictator Juan Perón. Borges was not primarily interested in politics, but he had criticized Perón's support for the Nazis and their allies. In revenge Perón tried to humiliate Borges and briefly imprisoned Borges's mother and sister. Then he took away Borges's library job and "promoted" him to inspector of chickens and rabbits, implying that he was a coward. Instead Borges turned to full-time writing and editing, and he even began lecturing on literature, despite his fear of public speaking. He became a hero to those who opposed Perón. After Perón's downfall in the 1950s, the Argentine government honored Borges, making him director of the National Library.

By now Borges was completely blind, but he kept writing by dictating his work to others. In his sixties, he suddenly became famous internationally when he received a major literary award, the Formentor Prize. Universities around the world invited him to teach. He received honors wherever he went, and was idolized by a new generation of readers. Unaffected by fame, Borges continued to dream, to write, and to be astonished by the world around him.

## BORGES'S ARGENTINA

Like many countries in South America, Argentina was once part of a huge area claimed by Spain. As in North America, European settlers in Argentina expelled or killed most of the natives, leaving little trace of their culture. In the early nineteenth century the territory containing Argentina revolted against Spain. After winning independence, it split into the countries of Bolivia, Uruguay, Paraguay, and Argentina.

With its rich lands and varied climate, Argentina soon attracted settlers from all over the world. They set up huge cattle and sheep ranches, farmed the pampas (plains), built railways, manufactured goods to export,

*Borges romanticized the lives of Argentinian cowboys, or gauchos, just as North Americans romanticize their own cowboys.*

70

*Borges loved the music and lyrics of the tango, a dance of passion, though he himself led a quiet life.*

and prospered. Spanish remained the national language, but other European and Asian peoples contributed to a culture that recognized many different backgrounds.

With such diversity Argentines have generally been tolerant of each other. They pride themselves on their high level of education and artistic achievement. Reading is one of their many passions, and writers deeply influence their thinking.

Argentines have suffered from unstable governments from the time they gained independence. Although Argentina's constitution was modeled upon that of the United States and human rights were guaranteed to all, the country has often been ruled by military dictators, making it impossible for any leader to survive without the support of powerful generals.

Juan Perón was such a dictator. He stifled many constitutional freedoms while buying popularity with social programs. Many Argentines adored his beautiful wife, Eva. After her death he tried to have her declared a saint. She has even become the basis for a world-famous musical called *Evita*. But Perón nearly bankrupted the country and was finally overthrown. Still, Perónism continues to fascinate Argentines, who have suffered even worse political oppression by later dictators.

Like that of many Argentines, Borges's ancestry was mixed. He was part Spanish, Portuguese, Italian, and English. He blended a European outlook with a pride in his country's heritage. He was fascinated with the romantic gauchos, the legendary cowboys of the pampas. He also loved the colorful language of the streets—*lunfardo*. A secret code-slang developed by gangsters, it substituted vivid imagery for nouns. For instance, someone's head might be called a ball or a roof. This language inspired not only Borges and other writers but songwriters as well. Argentina's famous dance, the tango, was born out of *lunfardo*.

In his writing Borges mixed these Argentine elements with references to literature from around the world, and with dreams and events from his own life. He was a great scholar, and he could write academically when it suited him. But then he would hide little jokes in his apparently serious essays. For instance, he would write a book review—of a book never written. He would mix up quotes from real and imaginary books. People would want to read these made-up books, only to find they did not exist. This kind of playfulness was part of Borges's way of expressing how our entire lives are made up from our imagination. We often substitute ideas for direct experience. Sometimes these ideas work, but they can also mislead us, making life seem unreal. Borges wanted people really to see, feel, and be astonished by their lives, whether waking or dreaming.

## THE BLIND POET

Imagine you are sitting all alone in a room. Warm sunshine streams in through an open window, and a light breeze stirs the curtains. A clock ticks in the next room. From outside, you can sometimes hear traffic, children playing, or footsteps. As you sit, the noises from outside die away. The sun sets, and the room grows cooler. Little seems to be going on, no moment stands out as special, but you are not bored.

Borges spent many days like this. He could tell day from night, but he could not see. Instead, he listened to his world and felt its changes through his other senses. He dreamed, composed poetry, remembered past conversations, and waited patiently for visitors. He did not mind waiting. It was part of the astonishment he felt at simply being alive.

# BORGES IN ARGENTINA AND EUROPE

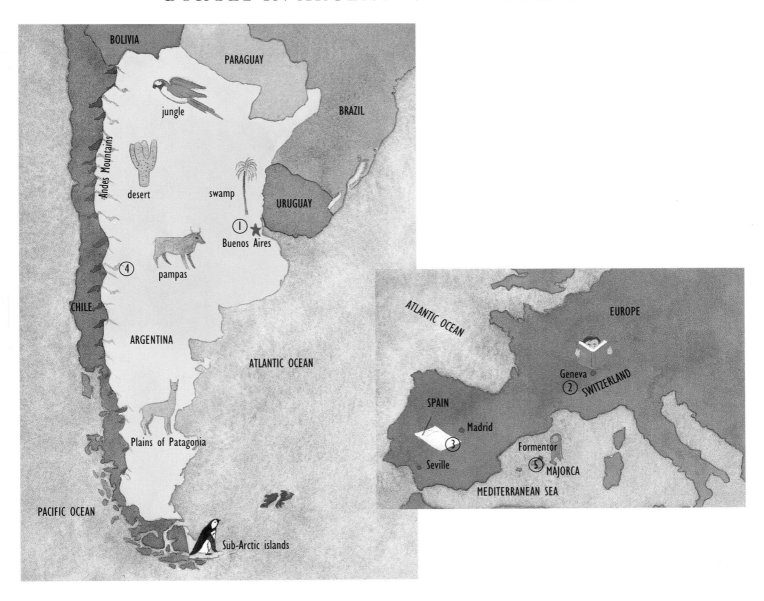

1. Borges was born in Buenos Aires in 1899, where he lived most of his life.
2. When Borges was fourteen, his family moved to Switzerland, where they spent World War I. There Borges studied languages and world literature, and developed a love of mystery and fantasy.
3. On their way home after the war, the Borges family stayed in Spain for a year. Borges became friends with a group of young poets there and brought their ideas back with him when he returned to Argentina in 1921.
4. In addition to European literature, the traditions of Argentina influenced Borges's writing. He became popular throughout the country, although he had to endure some indignities from the dictator Juan Perón.
5. In 1961, Borges and another author, Samuel Beckett, received the Formentor Prize, awarded by publishers from fourteen countries. He suddenly found himself famous and traveled the world, receiving additional awards and honors from different countries until his death in 1986.

# Martin Luther King, Jr.

*United States, 1929–1968*

Martin Luther King, Jr., was a hero of the civil rights movement in the United States. He led many thousands of people in nonviolent protests and other forms of resistance against racial discrimination. He raised black people's sense of pride while appealing to the goodness and sense of justice that all people share.

King was born in Atlanta, Georgia. His minister father combined religion with a sense of social justice. Throughout the southern United States, racial segregation had long been the law—black people were not allowed to go to the same school, live in the same neighborhoods, or even drink from the same water fountains as whites. King's loving family protected young Martin from some kinds of racism and made sure he knew that he was equal in worth to anyone else. Still, he grew up thinking the worst of white people, many of whom treated blacks with contempt and even cruelty.

Not until King went to college in the North did he realize that not all white people were racist. He decided that southern racism was kept alive by unjust laws that had to be changed. Then racist white people could overcome their mistaken attitudes. Blacks were already making some gains: in 1954, for example, the U.S. Supreme Court would declare school segregation illegal.

At college King also learned about Mahatma Gandhi's teachings of love and nonviolent resistance. Like Gandhi, he felt that there was no difference between spiritual longing and a desire for social justice. Gandhi's teachings showed him how he could work as a pastor to join these two ideals. Instead of staying in the North, King and his wife, Coretta, returned to the South, where they would work for civil rights.

Soon after he became a pastor in Montgomery, Alabama, King was thrust into leadership. An incident in the city sparked a nationwide civil rights movement. When riding on Montgomery buses, blacks could only sit in the back, and they had to give up their seats to whites on demand. In 1955 a black woman named Rosa Parks refused to get up and, as a result, was arrested. King and other black leaders organized a successful black boycott of the city buses that lasted over a year. The case of bus segregation went to the U.S. Supreme Court, which once again declared segregation illegal.

Nevertheless, governments of the southern states ignored this ruling. To push them along, King chose to follow Gandhi's methods of nonviolent resistance, which were based on

loving one's opponents. King and his supporters practiced civil disobedience in the name of higher justice and were always ready to go to prison, to be beaten, and even to be killed for their cause. They did not give in to hatred or try to triumph over white people. They believed that this approach would eventually awaken a sense of justice in their oppressors.

For the next thirteen years, King and others led people across the nation in nonviolent boycotts, sit-ins, marches, and demonstrations. As the civil rights movement spread, King raised the hopes and the pride of black people. His eloquent speeches moved both blacks and whites to join the crusade for civil rights. Together, they faced not just arrest but bombings, shootings, lynchings, and beatings by those opposed to integration. Shocked Americans watched as television broadcast scenes of policemen beating unarmed citizens and turning fire hoses and guard dogs upon them, and many demanded change. In 1964 the U.S. Congress passed stronger civil rights laws and began to enforce them.

*Even as newlyweds, the Kings knew the dangers they would face. After her husband's death, Coretta King continued the campaign for civil rights.*

Meanwhile King looked for the underlying causes of black powerlessness and poverty. He campaigned for equal education and job opportunities, voter registration, and a sense of black community and pride. He traveled tirelessly, working twenty hours a day, seven days a week.

Always the target for hatred, King was assassinated in 1968. His death seemed like a victory for violence, especially when blacks reacted by rioting in several cities. But King had never flinched from the violence he knew lay in everyone. He once said, "If you are cut down in a movement that is designed to save the soul of a nation, then no other death could be more redemptive." His dream did not die with him; today people continue working to make his "beloved community" a reality.

## THE JOURNEY TO FREEDOM

In 1863, in the middle of the devastating Civil War between northern and southern states, President Abraham Lincoln issued the Emancipation Proclamation, which outlawed slavery in the rebellious states. Although the North and South had then been at war for over two years, and although Lincoln himself opposed slavery, he had hoped that the South would end slavery voluntarily. But he finally realized that freedom for all would never be achieved that way.

After the Civil War, white southerners, defeated and angry, were not ready to alter their relationship with black people. Although free in theory, blacks soon found that little had changed. Whites still ran things, and within fifty years they had passed a series of legislation known as "Jim Crow" laws (after a white song-and-dance routine that demeaned blacks), which were designed to keep black people poor, ignorant, and subservient. From being forced to go to poorer schools to having to walk miles to find a blacks-only public lavatory and to being refused service in all-white restaurants, blacks were shut out of a normal life and kept from the prosperity many whites took for granted. Even in the North, black people often lived in unofficially segregated poorer neighborhoods.

Southern blacks were treated badly at every turn. For almost a hundred years after the Civil War, some whites tried to justify their attitudes by claiming that black people were naturally lazy or stupid. They contemptuously called black men "boys" and all blacks "niggers." Blacks felt keenly these harsh attacks on their sense of self-worth. Some of those who stood up for themselves only met with violence. In the South, white supremacist groups

like the Ku Klux Klan lynched and beat blacks, and bombed and burned their homes and churches, while police and judges looked the other way.

Even after the U.S. Supreme Court declared separate schools and buses illegal in 1954 and 1955 respectively, segregation was still widespread in the South. For instance, unless forced to integrate by federal troops, white politicians and police refused to allow black children into white schools. There simply were not enough troops to enforce integration everywhere.

*In 1963, young black children from Birmingham, Alabama, marched to protest segregation. Police set dogs after them and firemen sprayed them with hoses, sparking national outrage.*

Despite such obstacles blacks still managed to improve their lives and work for change. Martin Luther King, Jr., was part of a rising generation that was better off financially and educationally. His father had gone from being a penniless sharecropper's son to a well-educated minister through his own efforts. People like King felt an even better world was possible for their children, and they were willing to give their lives for that vision. They knew that while federal troops could enforce the laws against racism, only mutual respect and personal commitment could change the racism in people's hearts.

As the years passed from the 1950s to 1960s, King's philosophy was often attacked by extremists, who thought he was pushing for progress either too quickly or too slowly. It took all of his courage to stand clearly behind his principles of love and nonviolence. He often reminded his supporters to hate not other people but only their wrong actions. He firmly believed that all people had a goodness in them that could be awakened by confronting their fear and hatred. His philosophy and commitment earned him the Nobel Peace Prize in 1964. At the age of thirty-five, he was the youngest recipient ever.

## I HAVE A DREAM

"I have a dream" was a phrase from King's most famous speech. He gave it at the end of a civil rights rally in 1963, standing in front of the Lincoln Memorial in Washington, D.C. He had expected to speak to 100,000 people, but instead there were 250,000 people from all over the country. They listened to him spellbound, with tears in their eyes, as he painted a picture in words of a world where all people lived in harmony.

King knew how to speak from the heart and how to inspire the same feeling in others. He had grown up in a church tradition that allowed people to express their inspiration openly and joyously, and he used that tradition in his civil rights speeches. He had a beautiful, deep voice, and he used vivid images to describe his ideas. Some of his speeches came close to poetry or song. He often quoted other great thinkers in a way that brought their ideas to life. While he treasured his own heritage, he shared an even greater human heritage with the entire world.

As he grew older, King recognized the vastness of what he was trying to achieve. He saw African and Asian nations gaining independence from white colonial powers, and he saw the black struggle for equality as part of a worldwide awakening. He believed that a new world was being born, and his dream was not that any one race would triumph over another but that all races, religions, and ways of life could be appreciated as different expressions of the same human dignity. His dream still lives.

# KING'S CAMPAIGNS FOR CIVIL RIGHTS IN THE U.S.

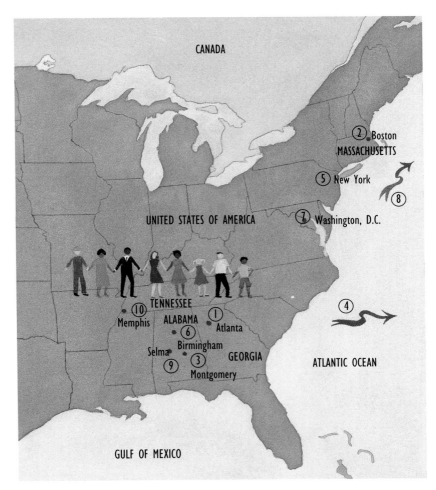

1. Martin Luther King, Jr., was born in Atlanta in 1929. He was ordained as a minister when he was only eighteen.
2. In 1951, after graduating from college, King moved to Boston to continue his education. There he met Coretta; they married in 1953.
3. The Kings moved to Montgomery, Alabama, in 1954, the same year the Supreme Court ruled school segregation unconstitutional. In 1955, King and other ministers began the successful year-long boycott of the bus system.
4. In 1957, the Kings traveled to Ghana and witnessed the growing independence movement in Africa. In 1959, they also traveled to India to pay homage to Mahatma Gandhi.
5. In 1958, while in New York on a book tour, King was stabbed and nearly killed by a deranged black woman — the strangest of the many attempts on his life.
6. In 1963, King led marches in Birmingham, Alabama. After he and all adult protesters were jailed, school children, some as young as six, marched in their stead.
7. That same year, King spoke at a mass rally in Washington, D.C., attended by 250,000 people from across the country.
8. In 1964, King received the Nobel Peace Prize in Stockholm. That year, Congress finally passed strong civil rights laws, and in 1965 they added a new voting rights law.
9. In 1965, after enduring beatings and arrests, King and his supporters from throughout the U.S. marched from Selma, Alabama, to Montgomery to support voting rights for black people.
10. King widened his campaign to include finding jobs and aid for poor people, black and white. He was planning a Poor People's march in Washington, D.C., in 1968 when, only days before it was due to begin, he was shot and killed in Memphis.

# Further Reading

Listed here are some books you might enjoy. The titles marked with an asterisk (*) are written especially for young people. Those with an exclamation mark (!) are my favorites.

## Socrates

*Bowra, C. M. *Classical Greece.* New York: Time-Life Books, 1965.

Green, Peter. *Ancient Greece: An Illustrated History.* New York: Viking Press, 1973.

*Mason, Cora. *Socrates: The Man Who Dared to Ask.* Boston: Beacon Press, 1953.

*More, Daisy, and John Bowman. *Clash of East and West: The Persians, Imperial Greece.* New York: Macmillan Publishing Co., 1980.

*Taylor, Duncan. *Ancient Greece.* London: Methuen & Co., 1964.

## Prince Taishi Shōtoku

Dilts, Marion. *The Pageant of Japanese History.* New York: David McKay Co., 1961.

Packard, Jerrold M. *Sons of Heaven: A Portrait of the Japanese Monarchy.* New York: Charles Scribner's Sons, 1987.

Reischauer, Edwin, and John Fairbank. *East Asia: The Great Tradition.* Boston: Houghton Mifflin Co., 1960.

## Mansa Kankan Musa

Atmore, Anthony, and Gillian Stacey. *Black Kingdoms Black Peoples.* New York: G. P. Putnam's Sons, 1979. Superb illustrations.

*Chu, Daniel, and Elliott Skinner. *A Glorious Age in Africa.* Trenton, N.J.: World Press, 1992.

*McKissack, Patricia, and Fredrich McKissack. *The Royal Kingdoms of Ghana, Mali, and Songhay.* New York: Henry Holt & Co., 1994.

## Leonardo da Vinci

Calder, Ritchie. *Leonardo and the Age of the Eye.* New York: Simon & Schuster, 1970.

!Clark, Kenneth. *Leonardo da Vinci.* Cambridge: Cambridge UP, 1952.

*Keele, Kenneth. *Leonardo da Vinci and the Art of Science.* Hove, Eng.: Wayland Publishers, 1977.

*!McLanathan, Richard. *Leonardo da Vinci.* New York: Harry N. Abrams, 1990. My favorite book on Leonardo.

!Reti, Ladislao, ed. *The Unknown Leonardo.* New York: McGraw-Hill Book Co., 1974. Excellent illustrations.

*Sachs, Marianne. *Leonardo and His World.* London: Ward Lock, 1979.

*Skira-Venturi, Rosabianca. *A Weekend with Leonardo da Vinci.* New York: Rizzoli International Publications, 1993.

## William Shakespeare

!Brown, Ivor. *Shakespeare in His Time.* Edinburgh: Thomas Nelson & Sons, 1960.

Fido, Martin. *Shakespeare.* London: Hamlyn Publishing, 1978.

*Martin, Christopher. *Shakespeare.* Hove, Eng.: Wayland, 1988.

*!Ross, Stewart. *Shakespeare and Macbeth.* London: Penguin, 1994.

Schoenbaum, S. *Shakespeare: The Globe and the World.* New York: Folger Shakespeare Library and Oxford UP, 1979.

*!Stanley, Diane. *Bard of Avon: The Story of William Shakespeare.* New York: Morrow Junior Books, 1992.

Wright, Louis B. *Shakespeare for Everyone.* New York: Washington Square Press, 1965.

## Benjamin Franklin

*The Autobiography of Benjamin Franklin.* New York: Franklin Watts, n.d.

*Daugherty, James. *Poor Richard.* New York: Viking Press, 1941.

*Davidson, Margaret. *Benjamin Franklin: Amazing American.* New York: Dell Publishing Co., 1988.

*!Davies, Eryl. *Benjamin Franklin: Experimenter Extraordinary.* Hove, Eng.: Wayland Publishers, 1981.

*Donovan, Frank R. *The Many Worlds of Benjamin Franklin.* New York: American Heritage Publishing Co., 1963.

Fleming, Thomas. *Benjamin Franklin.* New York: Four Winds, 1973.

*!Metzer, Milton. *Benjamin Franklin: The New American.* New York: Franklin Watts, 1988. Brings Franklin and his times to life.

## Wolfgang Amadeus Mozart

Downing, Julie. *Mozart Tonight.* New York: Macmillan Publishing Co., 1994. Written for younger children.

Hutchings, Arthur. *Mozart: The Man, the Musician.* London: Thames and Hudson, 1976.

*Komroff, Manuel. *Mozart.* New York: Alfred A. Knopf, 1956.

*!Krull, Kathleen. *Lives of the Musicians: Good Times, Bad Times.* San Diego: Harcourt Brace Jovanovich, 1993.

Robbins Landon, H. C. *Mozart: The Golden Years, 1781–1791.* New York: Schirmer Books, 1989.

## Sequoyah

*Coblentz, Catherine Cate. *Sequoya.* New York: Longmans, Green & Co., 1954. Fictional version of Sequoyah's life.

Malone, Henry Thompson. *Cherokees of the Old South.* Athens: University of Georgia Press, 1956.

*!Marriott, Alice. *Sequoyah, Leader of the Cherokees.* New York: Random House, 1956. Unusual account of Sequoyah's life.

Van Every, Dale. *Disinherited.* New York: William Morrow, 1966.

Woodward, Grace Steele. *The Cherokees.* Norman: University of Oklahoma Press, 1969.

## Mohandas Gandhi, the "Mahatma"

Coolidge, Olivia. *Gandhi.* Boston: Houghton Mifflin Co., 1971.

Gold, Gerald. *Gandhi: A Pictorial Biography.* New York: Newmarket Press, 1983.

*Rawding, F. W. *Gandhi and the Struggle for India's Independence.* Cambridge: Cambridge UP, 1980.

*Spin, Kathryn. *Gandhi.* London: Hamish Hamilton Children's Books, 1984.

## Albert Einstein

Highfield, Roger, and Paul Carter. *The Private Lives of Albert Einstein.* London: Faber & Faber, 1993.

*Hunter, Nigel. *Einstein.* Hove, Eng.: Wayland Publishers, 1986.

*Reef, Catherine. *Albert Einstein, Scientist of the Twentieth Century.* Minneapolis: Dillon Press, 1991.

## Jorge Luis Borges

Monegal, Emir Rodriguez. *Jorge Luis Borges: A Literary Biography.* New York: E. P. Dutton, 1978.

*!Gofen, Ethel Caro. *Argentina.* New York: Marshall Cavendish Corporation, 1992. Makes you want to visit Argentina!

## Martin Luther King, Jr.

*Clayton, Ed. *Martin Luther King: The Peaceful Warrior.* New York: Prentice Hall, 1971.

*Davidson, Margaret. *I Have a Dream: The Story of Martin Luther King.* New York: Scholastic, 1986.

*!Jakoubeck, Robert. *Martin Luther King, Jr.* New York: Chelsea House Publishers, 1989.

!King, Jr., Martin Luther. *I Have a Dream: Writings and Speeches That Changed the World.* New York: Harper San Francisco, 1992. King's speeches are easy to read and very inspiring.

*Milton, Joyce. *Marching to Freedom: The Story of Martin Luther King, Jr.* New York: Dell Publishing Co., 1987.

*!Shuker, Nancy. *Martin Luther King.* New York: Chelsea House, 1985.

# PICTURE THIS!

# At the Beach

Karen Bryant-Mole

Heinemann Library

Des Plaines, Illinois

1999 Reed Educational & Professional Publishing
Published by Heinemann Library,
an imprint of Reed Educational & Professional Publishing,
1350 East Touhy Avenue, Suite 240 West
Des Plaines, IL 60018

© BryantMole Books 1997

**Designed by Jean Wheeler**
**Commissioned photography by Zul Mukhida**

Printed and bound in China

03 02 01 00 99
10 9 8 7 6 5 4 3 2 1

**Library of Congress Cataloging-in-Publication Data**

Bryant-Mole, Karen.
     At the beach / Karen Bryant-Mole.
        p.     cm. – (Picture this!)
     Includes index.
     Summary: Simple text and pictures feature many things and
activities found at the beach, including animals, swimming, safe
enjoyment of the sun, sports, plants, and more.
     ISBN 1-57572-898-2 (lib. bdg.)
     1. Beaches—Recreational use—Juvenile literature. 2. Outdoor
recreation—Juvenile literature. 3. Seashore—Recreational use-
-Juvenile literature. [1. Beaches.] I. Title. [II. Series:
Bryant-Mole, Karen. Picture this!
GV191.62.B79   1999
796'.083—dc21                                    99-10783
                                                 CIP

**Acknowledgments**
The Publishers would like to thank the following for permission to reproduce photographs. Bruce Coleman; 4 (right) and
20 (left) Charles & Sandra Hood, 5 (left) Harald Lange, 17 (right) Janos Jurka, 21 (left) N. Schwirtz, 21 (right) Allan G Potts,
Positive Images; 8 (both), 13 (left), 16 (left), Tony Stone Images; 4 (left) Mike Smith, 12 (left) Lori Adamski Peek, 12 (right) Claudia Kunin, 16
(right) Darrell Wong, 20 (right) Darryl Torckler, Zefa; 5 (right), 9 (both), 13 (right), 17 (left).

Some words appear in bold, **like this**. You can find out what they mean in the glossary.

# Contents

# Animals

There are many different animals living on and around the **seashore**.

# Swimming

Many people like swimming in the sea.

Flippers help you to swim quickly.

A **mask** and **snorkel** allow you to see and breathe with your head underwater.

# Safe Sun

It is important to **protect** yourself from the hot sun at the beach.

Here are some
ways to stay safe
in the sun.

# Shells

You can often find shells at the beach.

Every shell was once
a home for a sea **creature**.

# Having Fun

People like to have fun
at the beach.

Which of
these things
would you
like to do?

13

# Full of Air

Each of these objects has to be filled with air before it can be used.

15

# Sports

There are many kinds of sports to play at the beach.

sand
yachting

windsurfing

surfing

sailing

17

# In the Sand

You can use these beach
toys when you play
in the sand.

Have you ever built
a sand castle?

19

# Plants

Seaweeds are plants that grow in the sea's salty water.

These flowers and grasses are growing in sand.

# Collections

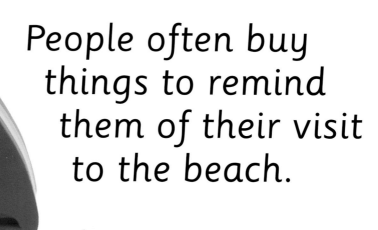

People often buy things to remind them of their visit to the beach.

They are known
as souvenirs.

# Glossary

**creature**  animal

**mask**  something that is worn over your eyes
   when swimming underwater

**protect**  keep safe

**seashore**   the land around the edge of the sea

**snorkel**  a tube that you can breathe through
   underwater

# Index

# More Books to Read

Darling, Kathy. *Seashore Babies*. New York: Walker Publishing
Company. 1997.

Pluckrose, Henry. *Seashore*. Danbury, CT: Children's Press. 1994.

# SIZES

**M**ost butterflies are small. But some species are large. Wingspan determines the butterfly's size. A wingspan can be less than one inch (2.5 cm) in some of the skippers and hairstreaks, to over six inches (15 cm) in the tropical species like the swallowtails and morphos.

Some caterpillars are large. While the large adult butterflies are pretty, large caterpillars can look scary!

**The spicebush swallowtail is a large butterfly.**

Skippers are small butterflies.

# SHAPES

**B**utterflies come in many shapes. Some, like the skippers, have fat bodies and short, stubby wings. Others, like the zebra longwing, have slender bodies and long, graceful wings with long tails on the lower wings.

Caterpillars have many strange shapes. Some are short and stubby. Others have odd eye markings and hairs that can be on the front, the rear, or completely covering the body.

Like all insects, butterflies have three body parts: the head, thorax, and abdomen. They also have six legs and a pair of antennae. These antennae are usually long and slender with a knob on the tip.

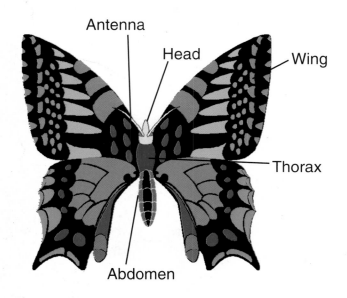

Antenna

Head

Wing

Thorax

Abdomen

**Top Right:**
**The caterpillar of the zebra longwing butterfly has hairs covering its body.**

**Bottom Right:**
**The zebra longwing butterfly has long, thin wings.**

# COLORS

**M**ost butterflies come in many colors. The morphos from South America are a bright blue. But some species are not so bright. Many skippers are very plain, which helps them blend in with their surroundings. This is called camouflage.

Many tropical species are brightly colored on the top of their wings, but are colored like leaves on the underside. When the wings are folded, the butterflies are hard to see on a bush or tree.

**Right:
A tiger
swallowtail
butterfly.**

# WHERE THEY LIVE

Butterflies need vegetation to live. Some species only live on one kind of plant, while others live on a wide variety.

Monarch butterflies and their caterpillars are often found on and around milkweed plants. Cabbage butterflies are attracted to gardens and fields where cabbage is growing.  Butterflies are also attracted to mud puddles, where they can drink.

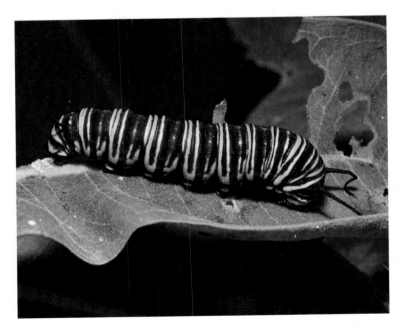

**Right:
Caterpillars have very powerful jaws that they use to crush food, which is mainly plants.**

**Left:
The caterpillar of the monarch butterfly is often found on milkweed plants.**

15

# SENSES

**B**utterflies have the same five senses as humans. Their eyesight is good and helps them find mates and the plants on which they lay their eggs. Butterflies can see things humans cannot. Their wing patterns can reflect ultraviolet light that is invisible to a predator's eyes, but not to another butterfly.

Their sense of smell is also good and helps them find plants for egg-laying. Some species migrate thousands of miles (kilometers) to Mexico, using their senses to find the way.

**This monarch butterfly has been tagged on its wing.**

Butterflies, like birds, fly south for the winter. Some fly as far as 2,000 miles (3,128 km) to reach a warmer climate.

# DEFENSE

Camouflage is an important defense. If a butterfly looks like its surroundings, a predator can't see it.

Some butterflies, like the owl butterfly of South America, have eye markings that make them appear larger than they really are, which will scare an enemy away.

Caterpillars may also have large eye markings that frighten enemies away. Others simply taste bad. Some caterpillars, like the spicebush swallowtail, have scent glands that give off a bad smell to enemies. These scent glands look like horns and only appear when the caterpillar is frightened.

**Right: This spicebush swallowtail caterpillar shows its scent glands.**

# FOOD

**M**ost butterflies will only eat one kind of plant. Others are not so hard to please. Adult butterflies drink flower nectar, using their long tongue to reach inside.

Some butterflies eat rotting fruit and tree sap. Forest-dwelling butterflies eat the sap from aphids and other plant-eating bugs. If you know what kind of plant a butterfly eats, you can often find their caterpillars.

**Right:
Adult butterflies
drink nectar from
flowers, using
their long tongue
to reach inside.**

# GLOSSARY

**Abdomen** (AB-do-men) - The rear body part of an arthropod.

**Antennae** (an-TEN-eye) - A pair of sense organs found on the head of an insect.

**Arthropod** (ARTH-row-pod) - An animal with its skeleton on the outside of its body.

**Camouflage** (CAM-a-flaj) - The ability to blend in with the surroundings.

**Caterpillar** - The larva of a butterfly or moth.

**Chrysalis** (KRIS-uh-liss) - The pupa of a butterfly.

**Ectothermic** (ek-toe-THERM-ik) - Regulating body temperature from an outside source.

**Environment** (en-VI-ron-ment) - Surroundings in which an animal lives.

**Habitat** (HAB-uh-tat) - An area in which an animal lives.

**Insect** (IN-sekt) - An arthropod with three body parts and six legs.

**Larva** (LAR-vuh) - The second stage of an insect that goes through a complete metamorphosis.

**Metamorphosis** (met-a-MORF-oh-sis) - The change from an egg to an adult.

**Migrate** (MY-grate) - To go from one region to another with the changing seasons.

**Nectar** (NECK-tur) - A sweet liquid found in many flowers.

**Order** - A grouping of animals.

**Predator** (PREAD-a-tore) - An animal that eats other animals.

**Pupa** (PEW-puh) - The third stage of an insect that goes through a complete metamorphosis.

**Species** (SPEE-seas) - A kind or type.

**Thorax** (THORE-axe) - The middle body part of an arthropod.

# INDEX

## About the Author

Jim Gerholdt has been studying reptiles and amphibians for more than 40 years. He has presented lectures and displays throughout the state of Minnesota for nine years. He is a founding member of the Minnesota Herpetological Society and is active in conservation issues involving reptiles and amphibians in India, Aruba, and Minnesota.

**Photo by Tim Judy**

## DATE DUE

| | | | |
|---|---|---|---|
| | | | |
| | | | |
| | | | |
| | | | |
| | | | |
| | | | |
| | | | |
| | | | |
| | | | |
| | | | |
| | | | |
| | | | |

595.78     Gerholdt, James E.
GER
          Butterflies

595.78
GER